Holocaust Survivors' Mental Health

Holocaust Survivors' Mental Health

T. L. Brink, PhD
Editor

The Haworth Press, Inc.
New York · London · Norwood (Australia)

Holocaust Survivors' Mental Health has also been published as *Clinical Gerontologist*, Volume 14, Number 3 1994.

The Haworth Press, Inc., 10 Alice Street, Binghamton, NY 13904-1580 USA

Library of Congress Cataloging-in-Publication Data

Holocaust survivors' mental health / T.L. Brink, editor.
     p. cm.
     "Has also been published as Clinical gerontologist, volume 14, number 3, 1994"–T.p. verso.
     Includes bibliographical references and index.
     ISBN 1-56024-669-3 (alk. paper)
     1. Holocaust survivors–Mental health. 2. Post-traumatic stress disorder–Treatment. 3. Psychotherapy for the aged. I. Brink, T.L. (Terry L.)
     [DNLM: 1. Stress Disorders, Post-Traumatic–therapy. 2. Holocaust. 3. Psychotherapy–in old age. W1 CL71D v. 14 no. 3 1994 / WM 170 H7546 1994]
RC541.4.H62H65 1994
616.85'21--dc20
DNLM/DLC
for Library of Congress

                                                 94-4500
                                                 CIP

INDEXING & ABSTRACTING

Contributions to this publication are selectively indexed or abstracted in print, electronic, online, or CD-ROM version(s) of the reference tools and information services listed below. This list is current as of the copyright date of this publication. See the end of this section for additional notes.

- *Abstracts in Social Gerontology: Current Literature on Aging*, National Council on the Aging, Library, 409 Third Street SW, 2nd Floor, Washington, DC 20024

- *Abstracts of Research in Pastoral Care & Counseling*, Loyola College, 7135 Minstrel Way, Suite 101, Columbia, MD 21045

- *AgeLine Database,* American Association of Retired Persons, 601 E Street NW, Washington, DC 20049

- *Applied Social Sciences Index & Abstracts (ASSIA)*, Bowker-Saur Limited, Maypole House, Maypole Road, West Grinstead, East Sussex RH19 1HH, England

- *Behavioral Medicine Abstracts*, The Society of Behavioral Medicine, 103 South Adams Street, Rockville, MD 20850

- *Biosciences Information Service of Biological Abstracts (BIOSIS)*, Biosciences Information Service, 2100 Arch Street, Philadelphia, PA 19103-1399

- *Cambridge Scientific Abstracts, Health & Safety Science Abstracts*, Cambridge Information Group, 7200 Wisconsin Avenue, #601, Bethesda, MD 20814

- *Communication Abstracts*, Temple University, 303 Annenberg Hall, Philadelphia, PA 19122

- *Cumulative Index to Nursing & Allied Health Literature (CINAHL)*, CINAHL Information Systems, P.O. Box 871/1509 Wilson Terrace, Glendale, CA 91209

- *Digest of Neurology and Psychiatry*, The Institute of Living, 400 Washington Street, Hartford, CT 06106

(continued)

- *Excerpta Medica/Electronic Publishing Division*, Elsevier Science Publishers, 655 Avenue of the Americas, New York, NY 10010

- *Human Resources Abstracts*, Sage Publications, Inc., 2455 Teller Road, Newbury Park, CA 91320

- *InPharma Weekly DIGEST & NEWS on: Pharmaceutical Literature, Drug Reactions & LMS,* Adis International Ltd., 41 Centorian Drive, Mairangi Bay, Auckland 10, New Zealand

- *Inventory of Marriage and Family Literature (online and hard copy)*, National Council on Family Relations, 3989 Central Avenue NE, Suite 550, Minneapolis, MN 55421

- *Mental Health Abstracts (online through DIALOG)*, IFI/Plenum Data Company, 3202 Kirkwood Highway, Wilmington, DE 19808

- *PASCAL International Bibliography T205: Sciences de l' Information Documentation*, INIST/CNRS-Service Gestion des Documents Primaires, 2 allee du Parc de Brabois, F-54514 Vandoeuvre-les-Nancy, Cedex, France

- *Psychological Abstracts (PsycINFO),* American Psychological Association, P.O. Box 91600, Washington, DC 20090-1600

- *Referativnyi Zhurnal (Abstracts Journal of the Institute of Scientific Information of the Republic of Russia)*, The Institute of Scientific Information, Baltijskaja ul., 14, Moscow A-219, Republic of Russia

- *Sage Family Studies Abstracts*, Sage Publications, Inc., 2455 Teller Road, Newbury Park, CA 91320

- *Social Planning/Policy & Development Abstracts (SOPODA)*, Sociological Abstracts, Inc., P.O. Box 22206, San Diego, CA 92192-0206

- *Social Work Research & Abstracts*, National Association of Social Workers, 750 First Street, NW, 8th Floor, Washington, DC 20002

- *Sociological Abstracts (SA)*, Sociological Abstracts, Inc., P.O. Box 22206, San Diego, CA 92192-0206

(continued)

SPECIAL BIBLIOGRAPHIC NOTES

related to special journal issues (separates)
and indexing/abstracting

☐ indexing/abstracting services in this list will also cover material in the "separate" that is co-published simultaneously with Haworth's special thematic journal issue or DocuSerial. Indexing/abstracting usually covers material at the article/chapter level.

☐ monographic co-editions are intended for either non-subscribers or libraries which intend to purchase a second copy for their circulating collections.

☐ monographic co-editions are reported to all jobbers/wholesalers/approval plans. The source journal is listed as the "series" to assist the prevention of duplicate purchasing in the same manner utilized for books-in-series.

☐ to facilitate user/access services all indexing/abstracting services are encouraged to utilize the co-indexing entry note indicated at the bottom of the first page of each article/chapter/contribution.

☐ this is intended to assist a library user of any reference tool (whether print, electronic, online, or CD-ROM) to locate the monographic version if the library has purchased this version but not a subscription to the source journal.

☐ individual articles/chapters in any Haworth publication are also available through the Haworth Document Delivery Services (HDDS).

Holocaust Survivors' Mental Health

CONTENTS

SECTION THREE: GROUP AND FAMILY APPROACHES

APPENDIXES

ABOUT THE EDITOR

T. L. Brink, PhD, is currently on the faculty of Crafton Hills College in Yucaipa, California, and Loma Linda University. He is a member of the International Council of Psychologists, the International Psychogeriatric Association, the National Social Science Association, the Western Psychological Association, and the Midwestern Psychological Association. The American Psychological Association named him a Distinguished Visitor in 1984.

During his career, Dr. Brink has developed the International Version of the Mental Status Questionnaire, the Geriatric Depression Scale, the Hypochondriasis Scale (Institutional Geriatric), the Scale for Paranoia (Observer Rated Geriatric), and the Stimulus Recognition Test. His books include *Geriatric Psychotherapy* (Human Sciences Press, 1979; Imago, 1983); *The Middle Class Credo* (R&E, 1984; Fawcett Gold Medal, 1985); *Clinical Gerontology: A Guide to Assessment and Intervention* (The Haworth Press, Inc. 1986); *The Elderly Uncooperative Patient* (The Haworth Press, Inc. 1987); *Mental Health in the Nursing Home* (The Haworth Press, Inc. 1990); and *Hispanic Aged Mental Health* (The Haworth Press, Inc. 1992). He has published over 300 articles, chapters and reviews. Dr. Brink has been the editor of the journal *Clinical Gerontologist* since 1982.

Introduction

The terms "Holocaust" and "Shoah" are used to describe the Nazi attempt to exterminate the Jewish people, and eliminate the Jewish heritage from world civilization. This effort had modest beginnings in the heightened persecution of German Jews in 1933, and grew into an attempt which was far more sustained and systematic than any of the *pogroms* devised at other times and places. The number systematically executed (or starved or worked to death) is usually given as six million. It might be higher or lower: the Nazis were more thorough in conducting the killing than in recording it.

The rapidly advancing armies of the allies liberated thousands of camp inmates who had undoubtedly been marked for death. These survivors have had a lifetime to cope with a variety of traumas: bereavement over the loss of loved ones, guilt over surviving when others perished, coping with the dehumanizing treatment at the hands of their captors, the stresses of immigration to new lands, and even the stigma they may have perceived afterward. Today these survivors are aging, confronting geriatric mental health challenges as a new layer upon the Holocaust experience. Some previous issues of *Clinical Gerontologist* have carried case studies of aging Holocaust survivors, e.g., 1984, III (1) pages 61-62; 1986 (VI) pages 11-13, but this present volume represents an attempt to pull together chapters written by mental health professionals working with this population in Israel and the United States.

The following chapters do not resolve some of the questions which I had advanced in my original call for papers, such as "Is Post Traumatic Stress Disorder an appropriate concept?" The

[Haworth co-indexing entry note]: "Introduction." Brink, T.L. Co-published simultaneously in the *Clinical Gerontologist* (The Haworth Press, Inc.) Vol. 14, No. 3, 1994, pp. 1-2; and: *Holocaust Survivors' Mental Health* (ed: T. L. Brink) The Haworth Press, Inc., 1994, pp. 1-2. Multiple copies of this article/chapter may be purchased from The Haworth Document Delivery Center [1-800-3-HAWORTH; 9:00 a.m. - 5:00 p.m. (EST)].

clearest conclusion suggested by the following research is that these Holocaust survivors demonstrate so much diversity in mental health levels and coping styles. These individuals were different people before the Holocaust, not only different from what they would be transformed into, but also different from each other. Therefore, they responded to the tragedies which befell them in different ways. *Defense mechanisms and psychotherapeutic interventions which work for one Holocaust survivor may be inappropriate for others.*

What was my interest in this project? Am I Jewish? In 1938 when a German official accused Charlie Chaplin of being Jewish, his response was "I haven't the honor." It was not just the Jews who went to the death camps. There were Gypsies, homosexuals, and a host of political dissidents, although Jews were probably the majority. When the history of the twentieth Century is written, the Holocaust will be seen as a crime not just against the Jewish race, but against the human race.

This book should be of interest to gerontologists and mental health professionals on at least three different levels. As social science researchers we are curious about Holocaust survivors: we want to observe defense mechanisms, psychopathology and intervention in a kind of worst case scenario. As mental health professionals we are dedicated to helping these now aging persons. *As members of the human race we must resolve never to forget, and never again to allow a Holocaust to happen.*

TLB

SECTION ONE:
MENTAL HEALTH
AND COPING

Holocaust Review and Bearing Witness as a Coping Mechanism of an Elderly Holocaust Survivor

Liora Bar-Tur, PhD
Rachel Levy-Shiff, PhD

EDITOR'S INTRODUCTION TO THE CHAPTER: Bar-Tur and Levy-Shiff present a case study of a survivor who is relatively mentally healthy. She maintains a high level of well-being via a frequent "witnessing" of her experiences. This active and public engagement serves as a kind of life review. The authors argue that although it may have started as the patient's attempt to justify her own survival, it has given her a sense of mastery and control which serves not only to find meaning in the past, but also helps her cope with the losses of aging, perhaps diminishing narcissism and sustaining an attachment to a wider circle of humanity as a kind of symbolic family.

This case study sets us on the right track: most Holocaust survivors are amazing and inspirational pictures of mental health, rather than pictures of hopeless mental illness.

Aging can be regarded as a phase of the life cycle requiring unique developmental tasks. It involves a wide array of changes,

Liora Bar-Tur at the time of this writing was affiliated with Psychological Services at Homes for the Aged, Mishan, Tel-Aviv, Israel. Rachel Levy-Shiff is affiliated with Bar-Ilan University, Ramat-Gan, Israel.

Address correspondence to: Liora Bar-Tur, Clinical Psychologist, School of Social Work, Tel-Aviv University, Ramat-Aviv, Israel, or to Rachel Levy-Shiff, Department of Psychology, Bar-Ilan University, Ramat-Gan 52900, Israel.

[Haworth co-indexing entry note]: "Holocaust Review and Bearing Witness as a Coping Mechanism of an Elderly Holocaust Survivor." Bar-Tur, Liora, and Rachel Levy-Shiff. Co-published simultaneously in the *Clinical Gerontologist* (The Haworth Press, Inc.) Vol. 14, No. 3, 1994, pp. 5-16; and: *Holocaust Survivors' Mental Health* (ed: T. L. Brink) The Haworth Press, Inc., 1994, pp. 5-16. Multiple copies of this article/chapter may be purchased from The Haworth Document Delivery Center [1-800-3-HAWORTH; 9:00 a.m. - 5:00 p.m. (EST)].

many of which are associated with physical and psychological losses. It requires complex processes of coping with one's past and present in order to accomplish adjustment and integrity rather than despair (Erikson, 1963). Holocaust survivors face an even more difficult task given their traumatic past. The present paper illustrates the use of the Holocaust review process and bearing witness as a coping mechanism that has enabled dealing with past traumas as well as maintaining mental health in old age.

Old age, with its multiple losses, imposes the inescapable necessity of facing one's past and forces a shift from doing to thinking, from planning to reminiscing, from preoccupation with everyday events and long-range planning to reevaluating one's life (Krystal, 1981). It implies reviewing the life one has lived thus far and coming to terms with it.

Life review has been suggested as a naturally-occurring universal mental process characterized by progressive return to consciousness of past experiences, the resurgence of unresolved conflicts, and the recall of pleasant and sometimes unpleasant memories; normally, these revived experiences are surveyed and reintegrated. An important component of this process is acknowledging and accepting previous choices ". . . the acceptance of one's one and only life cycle as something that had to be and that, by necessity, permitted of no substitutions . . . " (Erikson, 1963, p. 268). This process is probably prompted by the realization of approaching dissolution and death, and by the inability to maintain one's sense of personal invulnerability (Butler, 1963).

The empirical studies on the universality and effectiveness of the life review process have been inconsistent (Tarman, 1988). It is not clear whether it occurs to all subjects and whether it is always adaptive. For some elderly people, life review can serve a potentially therapeutic function (Newton et al., 1986). It can be helpful in dealing with painful and conflicted reminiscence, enhancing the subjective quality of life (Sherman, 1985). Group reminiscing can increase perception of personal control in coping with issues of current relevance (Hewett et al., 1991). Yet, for others, life review can be detrimental to their emotional well-being, if they are unable to come to terms with past events and failures. The consequences may be anxiety, depression, panic, guilt, obsession, severe with-drawal, or suicide (Butler, 1963).

Life review can be very stressful for Holocaust survivors, as it can evoke painful memories, guilt, shame or trauma-related fears (Horowitz, 1986). Affirmation of one's past seems virtually impossible. The quantity or quality of losses may be beyond the individual's capacity to integrate, as one's entire people and civilization perished. The reexamination of their life can reactivate dormant traumatic memories and produce intense pain. Individuals who have lost a child or mate during the Holocaust can revive a survival guilt, and some assume a depressive or penitent lifestyle, lacking the capacity for effective grieving and complete mourning (Krystal, 1981). Moreover, for survivors of the Holocaust, old age in itself is traumatic. They may experience the sense of abandonment, isolation, and loneliness common among aging people as a repetition of being shunned and dehumanized during and right after the Holocaust (Danieli, 1981).

Some survivors refuse to engage in life review, refuse to talk about the past when asked, and suppress any memory of their traumatic experiences. Others, however, engage in a somewhat different process, that can be regarded as a Holocaust review, rather than as life review, since it is focused mainly on reviewing the Holocaust period, dealing with painful rather than pleasant memories of the past. It involves also the unique role of bearing witness. This is manifested in survivors who publicly talk about their Holocaust experiences, publish their memories, write books and poems about the Holocaust, and engage in educational missions and Holocaust-related activities. Holocaust review can be for them an effective coping mechanism, which, like life review, is enhanced by losses and death. The confrontation with innumerable losses and unnatural death early in life have never been resolved. The inability to integrate the traumatic past, the unfulfillable need for continuity and immortality, and the fear of forgetfulness, have motivated them to a long-life engagement in Holocaust review and bearing witness. Whereas life review process helps to disengage from the past and achieve resolution and better integration, the Holocaust review and bearing witness for the sake of documentation can be seen as an ongoing, perpetual, but never-ending attempt at integration–to tame traumatic memories, to situate them within their own conceptual framework (Mazor, Gampel, Enright, & Orenstein, 1990), and to create a synthesis which does not exclude anything from the memory process (Friedlander, 1978).

Bearing witness by those who survived a trauma or a disaster has been explained in terms of reconstruction of memory which includes an effort to reestablish three essential elements of psychic function: first, the sense of connection, namely, the ability to create an organic relationship between present and past; second, the sense of symbolic integration which is the cohesion and the significance of one's life including traumatic events; and third, the sense of movement, namely, the ability to develop and change after the trauma (Lifton, 1967, 1977, 1979). Holocaust review and bearing witness may have additional functions: It may be an attempt to reconcile oneself with history, to warn others, to exact vengeance, to extract endurable meaning from what had happened, and to obtain reparation, namely, to be remembered by others is to have one's existence validated in a way that transcends selfhood and personal time (Merowitz, 1981).

In aging, bearing witness can also serve the task of renunciation. The renunciation of the external world requires the knowledge that we have done enough good and been good enough, so that it is all right to rest. Bearing witness and documenting the past is leaving a legacy so that the victims, the survivors, and the Holocaust will not be forgotten. It provides a continuity which is crucial to adult development and integration in late life (Bengston, Reedy, & Gordon, 1985). It answers the questions of the survivors "Who will remember me?" "Will the memory of my people and of the Holocaust perish?" (Danieli, 1981), that parallel the questions of aging persons "Who loves me?" "Who cares if I live?"

CASE STUDY

Engaging in Holocaust review and bearing witness can, therefore, help the survivors in their quest for meaning, continuity, and integration, but it can also contribute to maintaining a high level of self-esteem and a relatively strong sense of well-being during old age. To illustrate its usefulness as a coping mechanism in old age, we present the case of Mrs. M-S, a survivor of the Holocaust, who at the age of 92, continues her 50 years' active mission as publicly bearing witness. Despite her deteriorating health and advanced age, Mrs. M-S is in both thinking and doing, planning and reminiscing, preoccupied with everyday events and long-range planning and continues to review the past, mainly the Holocaust. It seems that her traumatic experiences and losses make it impossible for her to complete the process of mourning and integration and to disengage from her beloved family who perished in the Holocaust. They are still alive in her inner world. Nevertheless, she is not depressed, has a high level of self-esteem, and despite past and present losses has a relatively strong sense of well-being.

We would like to suggest that her well-being is achieved through the process of Holocaust review and the mechanism of bearing witness. These enable her to gain a sense of control and mastery by externalizing her inner world, using words and actions. Through her ongoing activities and engagement with the past, she can also avoid and control the feelings of helplessness and hopelessness imposed by the reality of old age and nourish her damaged narcissism.

For the past 20 years Mrs. M-S has been living in a home for the aged. She spends most of the day in her room, writing and reading. In the evenings she watches TV and reads a daily newspaper. She is interested in current affairs and often feels stimulated by an interesting program on TV or the radio. It gives her ideas for new poems which are her latest means of expression. Since her book was recently translated into English, she is now very busy sending copies and letters to prominent people in the world as a means of spreading the story of the Holocaust. These activities are carried out all alone. Despite her bad health and physical weakness, she is very independent and continues with her mission. She does not complain or ask for help. Despite her loneliness and advanced age, she refuses any help from the social or psychological services.

Although she is well known in the home and has many acquaintances, she spends hardly any time socializing or participating in the activities (except for lectures that she attends regularly) and she does not have any close friends. However, she is always ready to be interviewed about the Holocaust and her personal tragedy by students or journalists, especially those who can contribute to her mission of bearing witness. Her vitality and sharpness impress everyone.

Mrs. M-S is a sole survivor of a prominent family from Poland. Her life span can be divided into two different lives and worlds, before and after the Holocaust.

Before the war (1901-1939). Mrs. M-S was born in Tarnopol, a small city in Poland. Her family was well established and included older and younger brothers. Her father was an educated man and a prominent figure in the Jewish and Polish community. As an only daughter, she was spoiled and loved by all. She was very attached to her mother and admired her father. A competent young woman, she worked as a teacher and later on as an assistant to the principal of a Jewish school. She was involved in various activities in both the Jewish and Polish community, in education and the Zionist movement. When she was 22, she married Mr. M. who worked as a principal of a state school. They lived happily in Warsaw and had a rich cultural and social life. Their only son was born when Mrs. M-S was 24. He was a very talented boy, a top violinist and a source of joy and pride to his parents. Mrs. M-S was 38 years old, a mature, active, successful, and happy woman, when her life collapsed.

The war years and immediate aftermath (1939-1947). In 1939, when Warsaw was conquered, Mrs. M-S escaped with her husband and son to their family in Soviet Tarnopol. She first worked as a deputy manager of an office in charge of all the flour mills of the district, a very responsible job. She then found a job as a teacher in high school, where she worked very hard and was extremely successful and respected. The situation changed in 1941, when the war between Russia and Germany broke out. The first loss was that of her younger brother who was drafted into the Red Army and later on met his death in Siberia. Her mother was then shot in their courtyard a few weeks later and in the same week her father, husband, and son, who were taken to labor, were murdered. Her first reaction to the death of her family was, as she described it, a kind of hysteria: "The world rocked around me—bereft of all my dear ones—left along. . . . " At the beginning she wanted to hang herself, but the neighbors held her back.

However, the guilt feelings that she harbored against herself and others were driving her mad. She resolved to fast in protest against her fate. She hoped in this way "to die also and not be alone anymore." Later on, she wandered for days through the city and its environs, searching for her family's bodies. She managed to get permission to open the graves where many Jews were buried. Together with a few more survivors she personally removed bodies and identified Jews to be buried, while continuing her search for her family. "At that time, the cemetery became, for all practical purposes, my home. I had come drearily to the conclusion that death had skipped over me for one purpose: that I might bury the dead. I hardly ate or slept, but spent my time identifying and burying bodies." Finding the bodies of her son and husband made her sob uncontrollably and, as she describes in her book, "the memory of what I saw still lives with me today."

She later entered a state of "a kind of paralysis." She felt nothing; she ceased to exist. Only one obsession was reawakened: Jewish burial, and she became frantically busy with her mission: i.e., to find more bodies of her family and bury them in the Jewish cemetery. For weeks she searched for her father's body, obsessively checking every grave, looking at bodies, but in vain. Her guilt for not having found him persists to this day. A lifetime later, in Israel, she was able to eternalize the names of her family in an appropriate memorial. Photos of these memorials are hanging on the walls of her tiny room and also presented in her books.

When the decree to move into the Ghetto came, she joined her old aunt and uncle and two cousins. She was determined to care for the old couple; it gave her, as she says, some meaning to having been left alone. She also organized schooling for the children of the Ghetto and was constantly busy with some missions and activities. At the end, however, she was taken together with the remaining Jews of the Ghetto and transported in the "death trains" destined for extermination at Camp Belzec. Eighty young women were crammed in the wagon. She organized an escape and instructed the women how to jump from the train, but tragically, most of the escapees were killed. Mrs. M-S believes that she is the only one to survive. (Years later she wrote a book and a children's play about this escape to eternalize the girls.) She jumped from the rushing train and in spite of her wounds successfully reached the besieged city of Lvov. She describes her escape as a series of miracles, but there was a lot of courage, planning, initiative, and strength displayed when she was confronted with Polish people during this escape and until she reached Lvov. In the Aryan sector of Lvov she managed to hide out for two years. She hid in the room of an elderly woman, spending most of the day in the closet or behind the bed. Being immobile and totally helpless, she survived by drifting between her inner world (where she was engaged with her beloved, deceased family, talking to them, reminiscing, dreaming) and the outer world, with which she tried to be in touch through reading daily newspapers brought to her by the old lady. In the midst of hunger and terror, a very special relationship was formed and despite the helplessness and hopelessness, she again managed to find a purpose for living. When death came close, during room-to-room searches by the Gestapo, she was only concerned for the old lady. The only reason to keep hiding was to save her. Reading the newspapers was also a way to gain some control over her life by planning and evaluating the future events.

Freedom was gained in 1944. "I felt like a human being again, although not a whole one–the years of the Nazi conquest left physical and psychological consequences which I endure to this day." Mrs. M-S slowly came to realize that she belongs to a limited group of the "walking wounded" who are different even from the other survivors: "left without any close, immediate family, totally alone. She had again found a teaching job and worked very hard to earn a minimal living. Soon she found another mission: i.e., to save a cousin who was in a Russian prison. She was engaged with this mission for quite a while, risking her life and eventually managing to release him."

In 1945, Mrs. M-S returned to Warsaw, where she became involved in another mission. Her main interest was in ransoming Jewish children back from the gentiles and sending them to Israel. She was involved in organizing activities for teen-age children, preparing them for life in Israel. She helped widows and orphans coming back from Siberia where they had been deported by the Russians. At that time she wrote her first testimony of an eyewitness given to the Polish authorities.

Although she was suffering from health problems, she was busy day and night, living, as she says, for the sake of saving other families and documenting the horror of the past.

1949-1971. In 1949, she emigrated to Israel. There she realized again that "my future lay in my own hands" and there was none to help. After finishing the Ulpan, she fought her way to a teaching job. In 1951, she married a man who had also lost his family in the Holocaust. She never really loved her husband, but decided that it would be good for her to be with someone who respected and loved her.

Her love for her first husband and son never diminished and she kept thinking and dreaming about them every day. Five years later, her husband became very sick. They had no intimate relations since then, but for years until his death in 1971, she nursed and cared for him. She also helped him in his business, while continuing teaching. During all these years, she continued her mission of bearing witness. She wrote articles, taught students about the Holocaust, and told many others the story of her family. In 1958, confined to her home with a broken leg, she wrote her first book in Polish telling the story of her family and her escape. She also wrote a chapter in a book about the history of her city Tarnopol. In 1965, she testified at a trial in Germany against some Gestapo criminals, describing in detail the various actions in Tarnopol and Lvov.

In 1971, when she retired, she moved with her sick husband to the home for the aged. Soon after, he died, leaving her alone again.

1971-1992. Freed from the task of looking after her husband and the house, she became, at the age of 70, fully engaged in her previous mission: i.e., bearing witness. However, whereas before when she was younger she taught and educated young people directly, in her old age her way of communicating is more passive and indirect through writing books, plays, letters, poems, and articles in the newspapers. She is also busy with eternalizing her family and lately also the woman who saved her, investing time, energy and money in this mission.

Today in her early nineties, Mrs. M-S is still a very busy woman. She writes letters and poems. "These poems are not simply poetry," she explained. "Each one has a message, a task, to educate, to pass on a message." Writing for her is a source of pride and satisfaction. It is also a way to distance herself from other people and, as she says, a way to keep her independence so that she can write whenever she has an idea and inspiration without disturbance. She smiles in irony as she talks. The pain has never ceased nor is it easier as she ages, but there is no sign of despair. Hope for her can be gained in the future of Israel. She has also been engaged lately in philosophical thinking in attempt to understand what happened, not only to Jews but to all those millions who were killed. She believes that some powerful natural force is responsible for the Holocaust in an attempt to reduce the population in the world. The death of her family was accidental and the fact that she was saved was simply a miracle. Her comfort is in the development and prosperity of Israel, the young and strong generation of Jews in their own land.

DISCUSSION

Mrs. M-S is one of those elderly survivors who coped effectively with many crises and difficult tasks. Her survival during the Holocaust was not only a miracle, as she believes, but also required a lot of strength and initiative. Coping with the loss of her whole family and the total destruction of her life was a major task. Later she had to cope with building a new life in a new country, while living with the memory of the past and with haunting guilt feelings. Today, at the age of 92, there is yet another task–to cope with aging.

The question which is often asked is "what keeps those elderly vulnerable 'walking wounded,' as Mrs. M-S describes herself, alive, relatively healthy, independent, and not depressed?" Since aging can be traumatic for survivors who cannot achieve well-being through integration of past experiences in a natural process of life review, and since they have, early in their lives, already experienced losses and confrontation with death which required adaptation and a somewhat different process of coping with loss and death, there may be, as we suggest, a unique coping mechanism for some survivors. This is the process of Holocaust review manifested in the mechanism of baring witness. It focuses entirely on reviewing the period of the Holocaust and is, therefore, different from life review that covers the entire life span and brings out mostly pleasant memories. In the case of Mrs. M-S, this process started soon after the Holocaust and continued throughout aging. It seems that since it cannot bring full integration and as it also serves other purposes, Holocaust review never really ends. Through bearing witness, the survivor is preoccupied with a certain mission which is beyond simply reviewing the Holocaust and documenting one's past experiences.

Bearing witness is a purpose for living and a justification for personal survival. This coping mechanism implies that the person takes upon himself/herself a responsibility, a task to save the memory of those who perished. It is an active role of a survivor who fights against helplessness and hopelessness, guilt feelings, and unbearable pain, through effective mastery and control of words and actions. As Merowitz (1982) suggests, words can contain and tame experiences and the act of bearing witness can provide meaning and reparation.

Mrs. M-S's lifestyle has not changed all these years. She was a competent, independent, and active woman before the Holocaust and being a well-integrated and mature woman she could survive. Her coping style is that of independence and control. This can explain her survival and continuous fight. For her, life is justified only if she fulfills her mission. At the beginning, during and after the Holocaust, she took upon herself the mission to save people. In Israel, she continued her mission through teaching and continuous engagement with the Holocaust.

In aging she keeps on documenting and bearing witness. This engagement can help her deal with both the present and the past. She is able to live simultaneously in two worlds; therefore, the impact of present losses is reduced. Despite her advanced age and deteriorating health, she keeps on doing and planning. It may never be possible for her to rest and stop, since her active engagement with the role of bearing witness protects her from painful feelings, gives her a sense of continuity and eternity that she can't achieve otherwise as a lonely, childless widow. It also gives her a sense of control and some mastery at least over her inner world. It seems that bearing witness in old age is also a nourishment of some survivors' damaged narcissism. It is a source of pride, attention, admiration, and interest of other people. It may be the only love and care that lonely elderly people with no family can receive. Her inability to rest can also be a result of the fear that when she stops, not only will she disappear, but also her family from the past who are kept alive all these years in her inner world.

REFERENCES

Bengston, U. L., Reedy, M. N., & Gordon, C. (1985). Aging self-conceptions. In J. E. Birren & K. W. Schaie (Eds.), *Handbook of the psychology of aging* (pp. 544-593). New York: Van Nostrand Reinhold.

Butler, R. N. (1963). The life review: An interpretation of reminiscing in the aged. *Psychiatry, 26,* 65-76.

Danieli, Y. (1981). The aging survivor of the Holocaust discussion: On the achievement of integration in aging survivors of the Nazi Holocaust. *Journal of Geriatric Psychiatry, 14,* 191-210.

Erikson, E. (1963). *Childhood and society* (2nd ed.). New York: Norton.

Erikson, E. H., Erikson, J. M., & Kiunick, H. Q. (1986). *Vital involvement in old age.* New York: Norton.

Friedlander, S. (1978). *Quand vient le souvenir.* Editions du Sevil.

Hewett, L. J., Asamen, J.K., Hedgespeth, J., & Dietch, J.T. (1991). Group reminiscence with nursing home residents. *Clinical Gerontologist, 10,* 69-72.

Horowitz, M. J. (1986). *Stress response syndromes.* New York: Aronson.

Janoff-Bulman, R. (1988). Victim of violence. In S. Fisher & J. Reason (Eds.), *Handbook of life stress, cognition and health* (pp. 101-113). New York: Wiley.

Krystal, H. (1981). The aging survivor of the Holocaust: Integration and self-healing in posttraumatic states. *Journal of Geriatric Psychiatry, 14,* 165-189.

Lifton, R. J. (1967). *Death in life: Survivors of Hiroshima.* New York: Random House.

Lifton, R. J. (1977). The sense of immortality. In H. Feifel (Ed.), *New meanings of death.* New York: McGraw-Hill.

Lifton, R. J. (1979). *The broken connection.* New York: Simon and Schuster.

Mazor, A., Gampel, Y., Enright, R. D., & Orenstein, R. (1990). Holocaust survivors: Coping with post-traumatic memories in childhood and 40 years later. *Journal of Traumatic Stress, 3,* 1-14.

Merowitz, M. (1981). The aging survivor of the Holocaust–words before we go: The experience of the Holocaust and its effects on communication in the aging survivor. *Journal of Geriatric Psychiatry, 14,* 241-244.

Newton, N.A., Brauer, D., Gutmann, D.L., Grunes, J. (1986). Psychodynamic therapy with the aged: A review. *Clinical Gerontologist, 5,* 205-229.

Sherman, E. (1985). A phenomenological approach to reminiscence and life review. *Clinical Gerontologist, 3,* 3-16.

Tarman, V.I. (1988). Autobiography: The negotiation of a lifetime. *International Journal of Aging and Human Development, 27,* 171-191.

Denial and Acceptance:
Coping and Defense Mechanisms

Michael J. Salamon, PhD

EDITOR'S INTRODUCTION TO THE CHAPTER: While the previous chapter emphasized mental health via reminiscence, Salamon paints an opposite approach: denial. Although avoidance and denial have traditionally been viewed as immature defense mechanisms, these two oases suggest that these coping techniques are often used effectively by Holocaust survivors. The task for the therapist is to recognize when patients use denial, and rather than mount a frontal assault on what has been effective, respectfully work with the patient to make the defense mechanism more mature.

The study of defense mechanisms and coping styles is a flourishing branch of personality development. As in the question of personality traits, coping and defense mechanisms over the years have been explored to more accurately define them and determine the degree of their stability within individuals. In recent years it has been suggested that defense mechanisms are a direct outgrowth of personality configurations. Cramer, Blatt and Ford (1988) postulated that the two disparate personality configurations, anaclitic and introjective, result in very specific defense mechanisms. In the anaclitic configuration, the goal is to maintain interpersonal relation-

Michael J. Salamon is affiliated with the Adult Developmental Center, Woodmere, NY 11598. The author wishes to thank Etan Zellner for his extensive assistance with the research and preparation for this article.

[Haworth co-indexing entry note]: "Denial and Acceptance: Coping and Defense Mechanisms." Salamon, Michael J. Co-published simultaneously in the *Clinical Gerontologist* (The Haworth Press, Inc.) Vol. 14, No. 3, 1994, pp. 17-25; and: *Holocaust Survivors' Mental Health* (ed: T. L. Brink) The Haworth Press, Inc., 1994, pp. 17-25. Multiple copies of this article/chapter may be purchased from The Haworth Document Delivery Center [1-800-3-HAWORTH; 9:00 a.m. - 5:00 p.m. (EST)].

ships at the expense of self development. The introjective configuration aims to enhance self development while neglecting interpersonal relationships. Each configuration, in turn, has attendant defense mechanisms. The anaclitic personality uses denial most frequently, while the introjective employs projection. According to Horowitz (1976) the defense mechanism of denial is motivated primarily by the ego's need to protect itself from an overwhelming stressor. Similarly, Cramer, Blatt and Ford (1988) indicated that defense mechanisms may be conceptualized into a developmental hierarchy: the least mature defense is denial, identification indicates the most developed level of personality organization, and projection lies somewhere in the middle of this continuum.

Understanding this conceptualization requires a clearer definition of the defense mechanisms themselves. In this hierarchical system denial is defined as the denial of reality with an with an excessive effort to maximize positive and minimize negatives.

Projection is focused on the protection of self from an external threat. Themes of entrapment, pursuit and escape abound and there is a great fear of death. The individual using the defense of identification regulates his or her own behavior gaining self-esteem through affiliation and the delay of gratification.

Roth and Cohen (1986) explored the use of approach and avoidance strategies as a means of coping with stress. They indicated that each technique may offer beneficial means of coping. Avoidant strategies such as denial help reduce stress while approach strategies which could include identification allow for more rapid action. There is evidence that in situations viewed as uncontrollable avoidance may be the better coping mechanism. However, Roth and Cohen concluded that the real benefits of avoidance can be achieved only if the time spent in avoiding the stressor is used to provide the individual with the resources to mobilize against the stressor, thus, facilitating approach.

One of the more hotly debated questions is whether coping mechanisms are affected by age. McCrae (1989) using two community based samples of over 400 subjects concluded that there was no indication of any difference between middle aged and older adults in their use of coping mechanisms. He further concluded that there was no proof that older persons reverted to a less mature style of coping as they grew older. In a longitudinal study of some of the same individuals McCrae (1989) also reported that coping mechanisms are enduring and remain relatively stable despite increasing age.

Labouvie-Vief, Hakim-Larson and Hobart (1987) take exception with the view that coping and defense mechanisms change little during adulthood. In a study of 100 subjects ranging in age from 10 to 77 years they found that coping and defense mechanisms appear to remain stable only if age is the criterion for developmental change. If, however, ego level and stress are used as predictors of change individual differences in coping may be accounted for by variability in developmental maturity.

An interesting finding in this study, which the authors view as paradoxical, is that those individuals found to be more mature tended to use the coping strategies of reversal. These strategies consist of the less mature defense mechanisms of denial, repression and negation. The authors suggested that a defense mechanism of denial may be more mature in that it allows the individual to reflect on a choice rather than respond automatically. More mature individuals may be employing less mature defense mechanisms to respond to a stressful event in a more accommodating manner. As Roth and Cohen (1986) indicted, the use of avoidance to deal with stress may in the long run, function to facilitate approach. In a similar vein Koenig, George and Siegler (1988) concluded that "emotion-regulating. . . coping behaviors are strategies employed to maintain mental health during stressful life events and time periods." It would appear from this brief review of the literature on coping and defense mechanisms that avoidant and denial strategies are considered less mature forms of dealing with stress unless they are used to temporarily allow the individual to withdraw from an overwhelming stressor and use that tine to strategize a more mature approach and identification strategies. Thus, while denial and avoidance are less mature, they serve a useful, albeit temporary, function in more mature individuals.

SURVIVORS

If one were to assume this theoretical framework to be an accurate representation of how individuals deal with stress than in situations where the stress is so overpowering for an extended period of time, a specific form of reactions leading to the development of a series of patterned responses may develop. For example, in order to deal with the daily tortures of life in a concentration camp, denial may have been the most appropriate defense mechanism at the time. However, upon liberation from camp, survivor's could not return to their prior life-style. The stress of war, liberation and ultimate change and formation of a new life was a continuing series of traumas. These stressors may have forced the on-going need for denial in some survivors. If this means of coping became the fixed response pattern then it would be difficult for survivors to evolve into more mature coping mechanisms.

Holocaust survivors lived through years of massive victimization. The fears of victimization and the attendant feelings persist for many survivors today. Many survivors suffer a pattern of guilt (Goldberg & Haught, 1983) described as survivor's syndrome (Nadler & Ben-Shusan, 1989). Survivors have difficulty expressing emotions and externalizing anger. They are often socially withdrawn, suspicious, and have a great distrust of strangers.

At the end of World War II Holocaust survivors often found that society was disinterested in what had transpired and for fear of ostracism or simply for being different by surviving, many survivors chose not to speak about the terrible events they endured. Several studies show that the psychological impact of the Holocaust is still clearly evident in survivors (Fried & Waxman, 1988; Nadler & Ben-Shushan, 1989). How survivors have coped with these continual feelings and the defense mechanisms they have employed clearly contribute to their present emotional well being.

As we have seen denial is considered one of the least mature defense mechanisms. Yet, it is the one most often employed when stressors are the most overwhelming. Denial is also useful as an appropriate defense mechanism to temporarily allow the individual the time to explore the threat and ultimately employ a more mature coping style at a future time. Some survivors, however, seem to be locked in a perpetual mechanism of denial while others have been able to move on to a level of acceptance. While all survivors of the Holocaust suffer a variety of pathologies it would appear from clinical experience and anecdotal report that those individuals unable to shift defenses to a more mature level have greater pathologies (Kaminer & Lavie, 1991).

Many examples of individuals with discrepant approaches to coping with the horrific experiences of the Holocaust have been seen in treatment. For the purposes of this paper two women, Mrs. B age 64 and Mrs. S age 63 were selected to represent the styles of denial and acceptance. Both women are married to men who themselves are not survivors. Their husbands are employed in manufacturing industries presently in upper management. Both women consider themselves to be middle class and are living in comfortable suburban communities. Each has four grown children, all married. Both Mrs. B and Mrs. S consider themselves primarily housewives, however, both have worked part-time out of their respective homes for the last 10 years. Both women are survivors of Auschwitz, Mrs. B having been there for approximately one year, Mrs. S approximately 16 months. Both were originally from small towns in Eastern Europe and are the only survivors of their immediate families. In spite of their many similarities neither woman knows the other.

While there are many striking resemblances one should not conclude that an attempt at formal matching was done for indeed there are too many variables to be controlled. Rather, the similarities in background and life-style are useful to make the point regarding differences in coping and defense mechanisms.

Mrs. S. was originally referred to psychotherapy for a sleep disorder. Her physician was reluctant to prescribe an anxiolytic or sleep preparation as she reported occasional transitory sleep disturbances in the past, all having spontaneously resolved. Specifically she would experience primary insomnia and early morning wakenings that lasted three to four weeks at a time. During intake Mrs. S, being very forthright, provided a detailed history of her life experiences. In the process of recounting her history Mrs. S openly indicated some very important facts to help in her care. Apparently the sleeplessness was caused by nightmares and seemed to follow a cyclic pattern. "We were taken to the camps during the week of the first winter thaw." Every year, when spring starts Mrs. S has recurrent nightmares of being herded onto a cattle car and suffocating to death. Her dreams also recur in early summer. Like many survivors who do not know the dates of the death of relatives she chose one date to commemorate their passing. That date is early summer. Mrs. S also spoke of how she commemorates her own life. At holiday time, like many survivors, she insists that her entire family get together. After the meal is served she speaks of her experiences for just a few minutes. "It's important for my family to know, even the grandchildren. And it's also good for me." In addition Mrs. S joined a survivors' group, was active in her temple, and volunteered several hours a month at a local hospital. She described her social life as active "but not too active so I have time for my family." She also recognized that "talking about what happens helps me feel a little better. I know it was not just a bad dream."

Mrs. B had seen several mental health professionals over the years and was alternatively diagnosed as dysthymic, bipolar, suffering from a major affective disorder or a schizoaffective disorder. She had been on a variety of antidepressants for several years with no clear benefit. Her daily routine outside of the home was never appropriate, however, she slept only two to three hours a night and would spend all of her time at home cleaning. Her children described her cleaning behavior as "compulsive, constant and almost maniacal." Other than part-time work she reported a limited social life with no other activity outside the home.

During intake Mrs. B was guarded and resistant. Her responses were primarily monosyllabic and spontaneous communication was very limited. She did not volunteer any historical information. At the third session she became slightly less guarded. Recognizing that she was not native born, the therapist inquired about her arrival in the United States. She indicated that it was "after World War II." In response to a question about where she spent the war she said "It was hard times, but mostly at home." It took several more very directed questions until she finally admitted that she had been in Auschwitz for a year. Following this revelation she immediately indicated that she "never discussed that time with anyone and was afraid to even now."

It took two additional sessions until the topic of the Holocaust could be discussed again. At that time when asked about her memories of Auschwitz her immediate response was to say "I remember it had beautiful flowers." She sat silently for about five minutes indicating that she was attempting to compose herself, however, she finally began to cry.

Over the next few sessions it became clear that Mrs. B's behavior was predicated on avoidance of any stimuli that might cause her to reexperience any of her earlier traumas. She rarely read a newspaper, would only go to a movie if it was a comedy and avoided friendships with individuals who were themselves survivors. She also got into the pattern of insomnia for fear of having distressing dreams. Mrs. B's behaviors were clearly predicted on denial of reality, maximizing the positive and minimizing or completely avoiding negatives. Mrs. B, with time, began to recognize that her compulsion of house cleaning at least on a superficial level was a mechanism she used to help herself focus on present activities and avoid experiencing a dissociative state. She had constant periods of hypervigilance, occasional unprovoked outbursts of anger and difficulty concentrating when not focused on a specific task.

CLINICAL IMPLICATIONS

In reviewing the treatment records of Mrs. B and Mrs. S it became clear that both women were suffering from Post Traumatic Stress Disorder (PTSD). The fact that both women were having to endure a never-ending sense of mourning (Fried & Waxman, 1988; Nadler & Ben-Shushan, 1989) cannot explain the differences in presentations of the disorder. Mrs. S. had a significantly milder presentation of PTSD while Mrs. B's was more severe. The use of denial was minimized by Mrs. S. and employed only during periods of stress.

There are some survivors whose ability to focus on their background is enhanced by a sense of family and need to bear witness (Rosenbloom, 1985). These survivors appear to be using a more approach-directed style of coping. Even the partial acceptance of the trauma allows for the opportunity to work through some of the emotional consequences. Thus those individuals who have used denial for a limited amount of time and are able to then use more mature coping styles appear to suffer less. This is apparently the form used by Mrs. S. Mrs. B, though, seemed to have been trapped in a style that allowed only for denial. Denying the past on a conscious level seemed to have allowed her to function in the present.

This mechanism for repressing the trauma did not work as evidenced by Mrs. B's many referrals for psychological treatment and limited social life.

One may question why some survivors have what appears to be an inherent ability not to become permanently locked into denial. While the responses may include genetic or personality makeup or supportive family or social networks, the message for the therapeutic provider is clear in the case of Holocaust survivors. The trauma, being as intense as it was, never disappears. There is a constant need to work through the emotions. In situations where the survivor has already done much of the psychic work moving toward a more mature coping style as Mrs. S had, treatment can be brief and well-focused. In cases such as those presented by Mrs. B hard work and insight are required on the part of the therapist and patient to recognize the extensive, even pathologic use of denial. In Mrs. B's case, denial was not used as a method of accommodation ultimately leading toward approach (Labouvie-Vief, Hakim-Larson & Hobart, 1987; Roth & Cohen, 1986). It rather, became a method to totally avoid any direct evaluation of the trauma. When she began to employ more mature coping techniques Mrs. B's overall behavior improved significantly.

CONCLUSION

The research on coping styles and defense mechanisms strongly suggests that avoidance and denial lie at the low end of a hierarchy of maturity with approach and acceptance residing at the highest levels of maturity. Some of the findings indicate that mechanisms do not change with increasing age while others indicate that if source of stress for which coping is factored in it may account for a large measure of variability. From this review of two Holocaust survivors it is clear that denial is a strong and often used defense against PTSD resultant from the traumas of their experiences. The degree to which denial is, however, employed by these individuals varied greatly from two or three discrete times a year to constant. Still, if the defenses are breached in a supportive way coping can be impacted and defense mechanisms may shift to a more mature technique.

REFERENCES

Cramer, P., Blatt, S.J. & Ford, R.Q (1988). Defense mechanisms in the anaclitic and introjective personality configuration. *Journal of Consulting and Clinical Psychology, 56,* 610-616.

Fried, H. & Waxman, H.M. (1988). Stockholm's Cafe 84: A unique day program for Jewish survivors of concentration camps. *The Gerontologist, 28,* 253-255.

Goldberg, S.L. & Haught, E. (November 1983). Tales of unbearable beauty. *Contemporary Administrator,* 30-35.

Horowitz, M. (1976). *Stress Response Syndromes.* New York: Aaronson.

Kaminer, H. & Lavie, P. (1991). Sleep and dreaming in Holocaust survivors: Dramatic decrease in dream recall in well-adjusted survivors. *Journal of Nervous and Mental Disease, 179,* 664-669.

Koenig, H.G., George, L.K. & Siegler, I.C. (1988). The use of religion and other emotion-regulating coping strategies among older adults. *The Gerontologist, 28,* 303-310.

Labouvie-Vief, G., Hakim-Larson, J. & Hobart, C.J. (1987). Age, ego level and the life-span development of coping and defense processes. *Psychology and Aging, 2,* 286-293.

McCrae, R.R. (1982). Age differences in the use of coping mechanisms. *Journal of Gerontology, 37,* 454-460.

McCrae, R.R. (1989). Age differences and change in the use of coping mechanisms. *Journal of Gerontology, 44,* 161-169.

Nadler, A. & Ben-Shushan, D. (1989). Forty years later: Long-term consequences of massive traumatization as manifested by Holocaust survivors from the city and the kibbutz. *Journal of Consulting and Clinical Psychology, 57,* 287-293.

Rosenbloom, M. (1985). The Holocaust survivor in late life. *Journal of Gerontological Social Work, 6,* 181-191.

Roth, S. & Cohen, L.J. (1986). Approach, avoidance and coping with stress. *American Psychologist, 41,* 318-819.

How the Gulf War Affected
Aged Holocaust Survivors

Shira Hantman, MSW
Prof. Zahava Solomon
Dr. Edward Prager

EDITOR'S INTRODUCTION TO THE CHAPTER: Hantman, Solomon, and Prager present the only quantitative empirical research in this volume. Around the world we watched Israelis drill for poison gas, and then endure the unpredictable explosions of SCUD attacks. This must have elicited horrible memories of the Second World War for many aged. The authors herein report that aged Holocaust survivors differed in their reactions to the Gulf War. Those who had experienced prior war-related events were more vulnerable to stress.

INTRODUCTION

The Gulf War, in the winter of 1991, subjected the entire Israeli population to a state of emergency unlike anything else previously known in the country's history. Its proximity to the civilian population, the constant uncertainty of where and when the Iraqi SCUD missiles would land, the threat of unconventional warfare, specifically gas which necessitated the distribution of gas masks to the entire population, and the confinement in a sealed room each time a

---

Shira Hantman, Prof. Zahava Solomon and Dr. Edward Prager are affiliated with the Bob Schapell School of Social Work, Tel-Aviv University, Israel.

[Haworth co-indexing entry note]: "How the Gulf War Affected Aged Holocaust Survivors." Hantman, Shira, Zahava Solomon, and Edward Prager. Co-published simultaneously in the *Clinical Gerontologist* (The Haworth Press, Inc.) Vol. 14, No. 3, 1994, pp. 27-37; and: *Holocaust Survivors' Mental Health* (ed: T. L. Brink) The Haworth Press, Inc., 1994, pp. 27-37. Multiple copies of this article/chapter may be purchased from The Haworth Document Delivery Center [1-800-3-HAWORTH; 9:00 a.m. - 5:00 p.m. (EST)].

missile alarm sounded; all these combined created a sense of unrest and fear in the population.

The war posed particular stresses for the elderly who make up 14% of the population living in the Metropolitan area (the main target area of the 39 Iraqi missiles). With the outbreak of the war, social and health services went into emergency operation while local community services shut down, thus eliminating many sources of support for the aged. The sealed room and the use of the gas mask created technical as well as social problems. The sealed room shut off the aged from the outside world and the gas mask demanded a dexterity difficult for the aged.

Within the aged population one particular group's past experience strongly affected their ability to cope with the Gulf War: the Holocaust survivors. Ten percent of the aged population in Israel (Amcha, 1991) survived some form of terror inflicted by the Nazis during World War II. Certain aspects of the Gulf War bore a disturbing resemblance to the Holocaust. The passivity, threat of gas, closure in a sealed room, and Germany's involvement, all served as reminders of prior experiences.

AGING HOLOCAUST SURVIVORS

Although there is a great deal of evidence to the effect that Holocaust survivors, and especially aged survivors, are a vulnerable group, the literature still leaves open the question of how they would cope with stress reminiscent of the Holocaust ordeal. Does it impair their coping or might it make them better equipped to deal with hardship?

The literature on coping offers two contradictory views: the inoculation perspective and the vulnerability perspective (Solomon et al., 1987). The inoculation perspective claims that stress contributes to the development of useful coping strategies: that each stressful event increases familiarity leading to a decrease in the amount of perceived stress, enabling more successful adaptation in future stressful events. Eysenck (1988) refines this view somewhat, by proposing the use of both similar and dissimilar stressors. A stressor, he states, can promote either "direct tolerance" of similar stressors in the future and/or "indirect tolerance" of dissimilar stressors.

As applied to Holocaust survivors various authors have argued that the survivors are, on the whole, an emotionally healthy group (Leon et al., 1981; Lomerantz, 1990). Leon argues that only a minority of the survivors suffer the serious consequences to which other studies point (Antonowsky et al., 1971; Dor-Shav, 1978; Shanan & Shahar, 1983). Most live productive lives without major psychological impairment. Lomerantz feels that most survivors have succeeded in coping constructively and in achieving long-term adaptation.

The vulnerability perspective claims that prior experience with extreme trauma will reduce the ability of the individual to withstand additional stress. According to this approach, exposure to an extremely stressful event will reduce the individual's self-confidence and his coping ability with future stress-related events.

Literature has pointed to serious long-term emotional disturbances among Holocaust survivors. Niederland (1968) and Eitinger (1980) have identified the "Survivor" or "Concentration Camp Syndrome" as a state of chronic anxious, bland depression. Other symptoms include fear of the future, memory impairment, trouble concentrating, and recurrent nightmare of the trauma. These symptoms are recognized today as part of the post-traumatic stress syndrome (APA, 1987) that may afflict victims of any natural or manmade catastrophe.

Most studies of the long range emotional disorders of Holocaust survivors and their adjustment during and after internment have been based primarily on analysis of individuals who were seeking help for emotional problems (Choddof, 1986; Hodgkins et al., 1984; Dasberg, 1987; Dor-Shav, 1978). However, few studies have used non-clinical samples.

One such study was conducted by Shuval (1963) on a nonclinical sample five years after the liberation of the concentration camps. Her findings concluded that the concentration camp experience tended to induce relative pessimism among survivors as compared with "non Holocaust aged." A more recent study, conducted by Solomon and Prager (1992) during the Gulf War found acute distress, an enduring sense of danger, feeling of low self-efficacy and significantly high levels of State (acute) and Trait (characterological) anxiety among aged Holocaust survivors during the Gulf War. Since this sample was comprised of a group that had no reported clinical symptoms as well as a comparison group of the same ethnic and cultural background as the survivors, these findings are of significance. However, studies such as these are few and far apart.

It is possible that these conflicting views reflect different patterns of long-term coping. But, if they are a product of personal, familial and life-course factors (Lomerantz, 1990), or of specific traumatic events experienced throughout the life-span, then the cumulative effect of these events still remains to be answered.

In an attempt to provide a partial answer to these questions, a secondary analysis of the Solomon and Prager study (1992) was performed by the authors of this paper. They surveyed the impact of additional traumatic events on the response of the aged Holocaust survivors during the Gulf War. This study assessed the effects of two specific prior traumatic experiences on the anxiety level of a group of aged Holocaust survivors during the Gulf War: war-bereavement (parents who had lost a son in one of the wars fought in Israel), and war-related events similar to the Gulf War (air raids on Tel-Aviv during the War of Independence). Specifically, we examined the effect of these experiences on the sense of safety, symptoms of psychological distress and levels of State and Trait Anxiety.

METHOD

Sample: A total of 192 aged participated in the study. Due to the state of emergency during which the study took place a convenience sample was chosen based on two criteria: age–women over sixty and men over sixty-five; living location–the area defined by the civil defense as "Area A" having the highest risk of being hit by the Iraqi missiles. Forty-two percent were Holocaust survivors, 43% had experienced similar war-related experiences, and 20% had experienced war bereavement (some had experienced more than one event). The average age of the survivors was 68.3; 33.3% were male, 66.7% were female.

Measures: Subjects were first presented with a brief questionnaire inquiring about sociodemographic variables: age, sex, education, religious observance, marital status, place of residence, country of origin, and current health status. They were then asked about the nature of their Holocaust experience, namely, whether they had been in concentration camps, in hiding, or with partisan bands. This was followed by two sets of questions on other traumatic life experiences; specifically, whether they had lost a child in one of the wars fought by Israel and whether they had been exposed to other war-related events similar to the Gulf War. The subjects were then presented with four questionnaires which measured the following information.

Sense of Safety: Subjects were asked to rate their level of personal safety during the war in a number of different areas on a scale ranging from 1 (not at all) to 5 (very much). Internal validity of the nine item questionnaire was examined through factor analysis with varimax rotation. This analysis yielded three principle factors (eigenvalue greater than 1) that explained 62.6% of the variance. The first factor explained 31% of the variance and related to the subject's perception of danger. This factor includes questions such as "To what degree do you feel that your life is in danger?" and "To what degree do you assess that the country is in danger of being annihilated?" The second factor explained 19.3% of the variance and examines perceived self-efficacy. It includes questions such as "To what degree do you trust yourself to cope well at a time of danger?" and "To what degree will you know what to do during a chemical warfare attack?" The third factor explained 12.3% of the variance and contains items which examine the degree to which the subject trusts the various government and army authorities (e.g., civil defense) to protect against danger and to what degree the protective equipment (e.g., gas masks) distributed by the government will be effective.

Psychological Distress in Wartime: This self-report measure, devised for the current study, comprises 19 items all of which examine typical responses to extreme stress. Unfortunately, no standardized criteria for assessment of acute stress reactions are currently available, and even the most recent diagnostic and statistical manual, DSM-III-R, does not include a relevant category. The closest and most relevant nosological category in DSM-III-R is that of PTSD. The symptoms required for diagnosis of PTSD (e.g., distancing from others, nightmares, startle response, hyper-vigilance) were, therefore, chosen on the basis of most of the items in the questionnaire. Since this assessment was conducted during rather than after the exposure to the stressor, not all the DSM criteria were appropriate, and the criterion of one-month duration could not be met. For this reason no attempt was made to address the issue of diagnosis. Subjects were asked to rate the presence of each symptom in the past week on a four-point scale ranging from 1 (not at all) to 4 (very often). In order to examine internal consistency, Cronbach's alpha was calculated and was found to be high (0.90).

State and Trait Anxiety (Spielberger, Gorsuch and Lushene, 1970): This questionnaire is a standardized measure of anxiety that has been used frequently in studies of traumatic stress throughout the world, particularly with civilian populations, thus allowing for comparisons with other samples. The State Anxiety scale assesses the person's current or transitory emotional state, and the Trait Anxiety scale examines the way the subject generally feels. Both are composed of 20-item scales.

Procedure: In each community a local social worker well acquainted with the elderly residents of the area and experienced in working with this population was recruited to administer the questionnaire. The local worker approached potential subjects and requested their consent to participate in the study. Subjects completed the questionnaire in the presence of the social worker who answered questions as necessary.

RESULTS

Sense of Safety: To examine the effect of the prior traumatic experiences (Holocaust, bereavement and similar war-related experiences) on the eight items of the sense of safety questionnaire, a multivariate analysis yielded a significant effect for the Holocaust variable $F(8,125) = 4.18$, $p < .001$, with a significant interaction between Holocaust and similar war-related experiences $F(8,125) = 2.47$, $p < .05$.

A factor analysis performed on the sense of safety questionnaire yielded *two significant factors: sense of danger and self-efficacy.* A multivariate analysis performed on these two factors yielded a significant effect for the interaction between Holocaust and similar war-related experiences $F(1,139) = 3.96$, $p < .05$. The same results were found for self-efficacy. While for non-survivors there is no difference between those who had experienced prior similar war-related events and those who had not, among Holocaust survivors there is a significant difference between those who had experienced prior similar war-related events and those who had not; the latter showed a lower sense of self-efficacy and a higher sense of danger.

War-related Distress: To examine the effect of the three prior experiences on current distress a multivariate analysis was performed. It resulted in a significantly high effect of the Holocaust $F(1,142) = 20.53$, $p < .001$. A multivariate analysis of the interaction between Holocaust and similar war-related experiences resulted, once again in significantly high effects $F(1,142) = 5.8$, $p < .05$. Among non-survivors there is no significant difference between those who had experienced similar war-related events and those who had not; among survivors there is a significant difference: Holocaust survivors who had also been exposed to similar war-related events suffered significantly higher levels of distress during the Gulf War than those survivors who had not had similar war-related experiences.

State-Trait Anxiety: In order to test the relationship between prior experiences and Trait Anxiety, a MANOVA of the average score was performed on the three independent variables which showed a significant effect for the Holocaust experience, $F(1,138) = 26.52$, $p < .001$, similarly a significant effect for the interaction between the Holocaust experience and similar war-like experiences was shown.

Similarly, we repeated the above analysis on prior experiences and state anxiety. Once again, a significant effect was found for the Holocaust experience $F(1,137) = 10.01$, $p < .01$. However, the interaction between the Holocaust variable and similar war-like experiences was not significant. While for aged who had not experienced the Holocaust there is no difference between those who had similar war-like experiences and those who had not, there is a significant effect for those Holocaust survivors who had similar war-like experiences and those who had not. Trait Anxiety was significantly higher for those Holocaust survivors who had also experienced similar war-like experiences. This finding was not so for State Anxiety.

DISCUSSION

The findings of this study indicate that though aged Holocaust survivors suffered considerable emotional distress during the Gulf War (Solomon & Prager, 1992) there is great diversity in the vulnerability of this group. The study indicated significant differences in stress reactions between the group of survivors who had been previously exposed to similar war-related experiences and the groups of survivors who had not been exposed or who had suffered war bereavement prior to the Gulf War.

Higher levels of distress were reported by the former group as reflected in (1) sense of safety, (2) war-related distress and (3) trait anxiety. With regard to sense of safety, results indicated that survivors with prior war-related experiences reported a higher sense of danger and a lower self-efficacy during the Gulf War. This group also reported a sense of real threat on their lives and on the lives of their families. Furthermore, they felt unsure of being able to cope in the event of direct danger of a chemical attack.

Similarly, a significantly high level of war-related distress was reported by this group. This was manifested by tension, startle response, panic and fear, and a marked sense of hopelessness.

Finally, survivors who had also been exposed to similar war-related experiences prior to the Gulf War rated high in trait anxiety.

In other words, *Holocaust survivors who had undergone prior similar war-related experiences were found to be more vulnerable than other Holocaust survivors.* This finding does not support the view that prior exposure to extreme stress has an inoculating effect on an individual's coping ability with future adversity. In contrast with the Norris and Murrel (1988) study of the effect of re-exposure to another flood that found an inoculating effect, there was no such evidence in the present study. Furthermore, whereas they reported a higher resilience for both similar (direct-tolerance) and dissimilar (indirect-tolerance) events, the reverse was found to be true for aged Holocaust survivors: a higher sense of danger, lower self-efficacy, higher level of distress and trait anxiety was reported by aged survivors who had prior exposure to similar war-related experiences (direct-tolerance) than by survivors who had prior exposure to war-related bereavement (indirect tolerance). This finding is substantiated by the clinical observations of Emanuel Berman and was given empirical validity in research performed by the Israel Defense Forces regarding soldiers suffering from Combat Stress reaction (Solomon et al., 1990). Their findings report that re-exposure to trauma does not enable a "corrective experience" but rather that trauma deepens trauma. Moreover, the greater the similarity between two traumatic events, the greater the chance for reactivation of the original stress response following the second event (Solomon et al., 1987).

In relation to aged survivors of the Holocaust they have had to cope with multiple life events and stressors throughout their lifespan. Furthermore, they had to face normal developmental tasks of the aging process such as retirement or widowhood which were likely to pose additional stress (Christenson et al., 1981; Nicols & Czirr, 1986). However, these differential influences will have a diverse effect on the coping ability of survivors. This is given empirical validity in the literature reviewing the long-term psychological consequences of the Holocaust (e.g., Dasberg, 1987; Eitinger, 1980; Hodgkins et al., 1984).

As noted earlier, few studies of Holocaust survivors have used non-clinical populations. Most research has focused on physical and mental health problems of survivors seeking professional help (Krystal, 1968). Thus, the findings of the present community based study regarding acute stress and high levels of trait anxiety are significant. They reflect a non-clinical sample similar to the control group in ethnic and cultural background.

This study presents findings that point to the existence of a subgroup within the larger group of Holocaust survivors who reacted with a higher level of distress than the rest. This finding raises the need for a differentiation between the various groups of survivors based on their additional experiences over the life-span.

These findings have implications on preventive intervention during normative and traumatic crisis. In considering post-traumatic adaptation of aged Holocaust survivors, data reveals that the enduring response appears to be continued perception of threat in the environment (Kahana et al., 1988). Thus, we see the importance of developing on-going special support programs both formal and informal which will answer the specific needs of this particular population.

These programs should be preventive in nature, enabling survivor accessibility in daily needs, reinforced in times of unusual traumatic events such as war. The fact that aged Holocaust survivors exist in a state of chronic distress strengthens the need for a service that will provide short term treatment, which provides the survivor with an environment in which he feels accepted and enables him to receive legitimization of his feelings and fears. This sort of service might lessen the sense of helplessness when confronted with daily hassles in general and with extreme stress in particular.

REFERENCES

Amcha (1991). Report of the National Israeli Center for Psychosocial Support of Survivors of Holocaust and the Second Generation.

Antonowsky, A., Maoz, B. et al. (1971). Twenty five years later: A limited study of sequelae of the concentration camp experience, *Social Psychiatry*, *6*: 186-193.

American Psychiatric Association (1987). *Diagnostic and Statistical Manual of Mental Disorders-DSM-III-R*. Washington D.C.

Chodoff, P. (1986). Survivors of the Nazi Holocaust. In Moos, R. (Ed), *Coping With Life Crisis*, New York: Plenum Press, pp. 407-415.

Christenson, R.M. et al. (1981). Reactivation of Traumatic Conflicts, *American Journal of Psychiatry*, *138*: 984-985.

Dasberg, H. (1987). Psychological Distress of Holocaust Survivors and their Offspring in Israel, Forty Years Later: A Review, *Israel Journal of Psychiatry and Related Sciences*, *24*: 243-256.

Dor-Shav, N.K. (1978). On the long-range effects of concentration camp internment of Nazi victims: 25 years later, *Journal of Consulting and Clinical Psychiatry*, *46*: 1-11.

Eitinger, L. (1980). The Concentration Camp Syndrome and its Late Sequelae. In Dimsdale, J. (Ed.), *Survivors, Victims and Perpetrators*, Hemisphere Pub. Co.

Eysenck, H. J. (1988). Stress, Disease, and Personality: The Inoculation Effect. In C.L. Cooper (Ed.), *Stress Research*, New York: John Wiley & Sons. pp. 121-146.

Hodgkins, B. J., & Douglass, M. P. H. (1984). Research Issues Surrounding Holocaust Survivors, *Journal of Society and Social Welfare*, *11*: 894-914.

Kahana, E., Kahana, B., Harel, Z., & Rosner, T. (1988). Coping with extreme trauma. In, J. Wilson, Z. Harel, & B. Kahana (Eds.), *Human Adaptation to Extreme Stress: From the Holocaust to Vietnam*. New York: Plenum Press. pp. 55-79.

Krystal, H. (1968). *Massive Psychic Trauma*. New York: International Universities Press.

Leon, G. R., Butcher, J. N., & Kleinman, M. et al., (1981). Survivors of the Holocaust and their children: current status and adjustment, *Journal Personality and Social Psychology, 41*: 503-506.

Lomerantz, J. (1990). Long-term adaptation to traumatic stress in light of adult development and aging perspectives. In, M. A. Stephens, Crowther, S. Hobfoll, & Tennebaum (Eds)., *Stress and Coping in Life families*, Washington D.C.: Hemisphere Pub, pp. 99-121.

Neiderland, W.G. (1968). The problem of the survivor. In, H. Krystal (Ed)., *Massive Psychic Trauma*. New York: International Universities Press.

Nicols, B., & Czirr, R. (1986). Post-Traumatic Stress Disorder: Hidden syndrome in Elders, *Clinical Gerontologist, 5*: 417-433.

Norris, F. H., & Murrel, S. A. (1988). Prior Experience as a Moderator of Disaster Impact on Anxiety Symptoms in Older Adults, *American Journal of Community Psychology, 16*: 665-683.

Shanan, J., & Shahar, O. (1983). Cognitive and Personality Functioning of Jewish Holocaust Survivors During Midlife Transition in Israel, *Archives of Psychology, 135*: 275-294.

Shuval, Y. (1963). The Concentration Camp. In, Y. Shuval (Ed.), *Immigrants on the Threshold*. New York: Atherton Press, pp. 79-103.

Solomon, Z., Oppenheimer, B., Elizur, Y., & Waysman, M. (1990). Exposure to recurrent combat stress: Can successful coping in a second war heal combat-related PTSD from the past? *Journal of Anxiety Disorders, 4*: 141-145.

Solomon, Z., Garb, R., Bleich, A., Gruper, D. (1987). Reactivation of combat related Post Traumatic Stress Disorder, *American Journal of Psychiatry, 144*: 51-55.

Solomon, Z. & Prager, E. (1992). Elderly Israeli Holocaust Survivors during the Persian Gulf war: A study of psychological distress, *American Journal of Psychiatry, 149*: 1707-1710.

Spielberger, C. D., Gorsuch, R. L. & Lushene, R. E. (1970). *Manual for the State-Trait Anxiety Inventory*, Palo Alto: California, Consulting Psychologists Press.

SECTION TWO:
ISSUES AND TECHNIQUES
IN INDIVIDUAL TREATMENT

Paranoid Psychosis
in a Holocaust Survivor

Pesach Lichtenberg, MD
Esther-Lee Marcus, MD

EDITOR'S INTRODUCTION TO THE CHAPTER: Lichtenberg and Marcus present a case study of an 85 year old man with paranoid delusions. This case demonstrates the importance of assessing each patient thoroughly, and coming up with a treatment plan appropriateness to the unique constraints and opportunities therein presented. In general, insight therapy would be less appropriate in geriatric paranoia, while supportive therapy would be recommended.

INTRODUCTION

The aging Holocaust survivor suffering from psychotic illness presents special problems for the treating psychiatrist. The patient has experienced a profound, extended existential threat; he is beset with the common emotional struggles of late life; and his sense of reality is askew. Accordingly, treatment must be adapted to the multifaceted needs of the patient.

We describe here a case where all of these elements were present in the patient and needed to be addressed by his physicians.

Pesach Lichtenberg is affiliated with the Psychiatry Department and Esther-Lee Marcus is affiliated with the Geriatric Department at the Sarah Herzog Memorial Hospital, P.O. Box 35300, Jerusalem, 91351, Israel.

[Haworth co-indexing entry note]: "Paranoid Psychosis in a Holocaust Survivor." Lichtenberg, Pesach and Esther-Lee Marcus. Co-published simultaneously in the *Clinical Gerontologist* (The Haworth Press, Inc.) Vol. 14, No. 3, 1994, pp. 41-46; and: *Holocaust Survivors' Mental Health* (ed: T. L. Brink) The Haworth Press, Inc., 1994, pp. 41-46. Multiple copies of this article/chapter may be purchased from The Haworth Document Delivery Center [1-800-3-HAWORTH; 9:00 a.m. - 5:00 p.m. (EST)].

CASE REPORT

Anshel, an 85-year-old Polish-born divorced man, was admitted to the Psychiatric Department of the Herzog Hospital, a combined Psychiatric and Geriatric Hospital. He was in an agitated state and protested vigorously that he was being molested by neighbors who had been recruited for such malignant purposes by the "Communist mafia."

Anshel was known to us from several previous hospitalizations over the past 15 years. He grew up in a traditional Jewish family as one of ten children. Before the Second World War, he lived in a small town in Galicia, Poland, and supported his family by working at a small tailor shop he owned. When the Germans invaded, he fled eastward with his wife and four year old daughter into Russian-occupied Poland. When this area, too, was overrun by the Wehrmacht, he realized that his only chance for survival was to escape into hiding. Amidst the confusion, he was separated from his family. He spent the next two years alone in a subterranean hideout, daring to forage the forest for food only at night. When the German retreat at last allowed him to reenter the world, be learnt that his wife and daughter had perished, along with all but one of his siblings.

Anshel remarried after the war and remained in Poland, eventually emigrating to Israel in the 1960s. Shortly thereafter he separated from his wife.

In retrospect, Anshel appears to have already embarked upon his delusional pursuits during this period. He believes that an errant remark he uttered at the barbershop to the effect that life had been difficult under the Polish regime ignited an international campaign against him, masterminded by "the Polish Communist mafia." He has focused much of his energy these past twenty years compiling dossiers attesting to his victimization. The evidence was everywhere to be found: neighbors making noise at night, bureaucrats acting impolitely, police ignoring his repeated pleas for protection. Letters petitioning public figures brought no response. According to his delusions, the tentacles of the "Communist mafia" reached into the upper echelons of society.

Anshel was hospitalized three times in the past, usually for several months. He typically responded to pharmacotherapy (haloperidol or chlorpromazine), and was released home. On his own, he would stop his medication and resume his investigations. When his neighbors found his renewed invectives intolerable, and after he punctuated his threats of retaliation by casting excrement-filled bottles at his neighbors entrances, Anshel was rehospitalized.

Upon admission, Anshel appeared in disarray as he denounced his numerous enemies. He defiantly and energetically enumerated their many misdeeds against him. Despite his wizened visage, age seemed not only to have failed to mellow him, but to have actually heightened the intensity of his rage.

In the absence of hallucinations and bizarre delusions, Anshel was diagnosed as suffering from delusional disorder, paranoid type, in accord with DSM-III-I (American Psychiatric Association, 1987).

A home visit demonstrated further how desperate his delusions made him. Plywood was tacked onto his walls to prevent his neighbors from sending poison gas into his home. His bed was chained to the door to prevent enemy infiltration.

At the hospital, Anshel was placed on an open ward (a closed ward seemed not only superfluous, but potentially too reminiscent of past traumas). He cooperated with the staff, though he demonstrated a tendency to "split" between staff members perceived as good or bad. Indeed, the defense mechanism of splitting seemed quite prominent in his psychological repertoire; for example, when describing his neighbors, he stated, "The neighbors to my right, well, they are simply angels, wonderful people, but those on the other side—they're Gestapo!"

Treatment was started with a small dose of haloperidol (2 mg) per os daily. In addition, he was placed in group and individual psychotherapy. Within several days, Anshel was considerably calmer, though he adhered to his delusional system, and flaunted the letters documenting his fruitless correspondence with the authorities.

Gradually, the content of Anshel's tales turned from his tribulations at the hands of the communist mafia to his experiences in hiding from the Nazis. He described his close encounters evading Nazi soldiers and local citizens all too eager to discover a Jew in hiding.

The psychotherapist decided that an insight-oriented approach was not indicated, in light of Anshel's age, his difficulty with introspection, and the intensity of the fears lurking behind his projective defense mechanisms. Rather than attempting to interpret or reconstruct Anshel's defenses and personality, stress was laid upon allowing him to relate his experiences at his own pace.

For example, when a nurse mistakenly placed Anshel's pants with the collective laundry, Anshel went into a rage, accusing the nurse of working together with the Nazis. The nurse, who had been made aware of Anshel's special history and sensitivity, apologized, and Anshel became calmer. He was then able to relate more of his underground experiences, such as the difficulty in procuring even the most basic clothing to survive the winter.

Significantly, during his two-month hospitalization, Anshel never spoke of his lost family; and when asked about life prior to the war he would answer perfunctorily and dryly without revealing much information.

In contrast, Anshel clearly enjoyed the ability to tell of his experiences during the war and looked forward to these opportunities. He became quite comfortable on the ward, and while he never completely relinquished his delusional conspiracy theories, they certainly subsided in intensity sufficiently to allow for his eventual discharge.

We were concerned that Anshel's return home would lead to the resumption of his prior difficulties with neighbors. We considered conducting a home visit prior to discharge in order to speak with them, in the hope of encouraging their understanding and patience. However, following the advice of a social worker familiar with his home situation, we decided against that option for fear of inadvertently arousing among his neighbors resistance to his return. Ultimately, our concerns were allayed when we brought up the subject with Anshel. He assured us that his neighbors had been replaced by more friendly types.

At six month ambulatory follow-up, Anshel remains well. He is still prepared to rail against the injustices inflicted upon him by various imagined adversaries. However these delusions are not central to his life, which he manages to lead quietly, tending independently to his needs and living at peace with his neighbors.

DISCUSSION

We have presented here the difficult case of a survivor of the Holocaust who continues to be hounded by ghosts from the past. The treatment goals were limited, and partially achieved via a combination of pharmacotherapy and supportive psychotherapy.

According to Erikson's (1963) epigenetic scheme of human development, the aging individual may achieve integrity–an acceptance of one's life, with its various accomplishments and failures–or despair. Achieving the former requires the successful navigation of life's earlier stages. A Holocaust victim such as Anshel fails to attain or, following his traumatic experiences, to maintain even the earliest developmental milestone, that of basic trust (Chodoff, 1980). This block may lead to apathy or depression; in Anshel's case, it may have promoted the development of a paranoid psychosis.

That Anshel's psychosis erupted relatively late in life is of interest. Danieli's comment (1981) is relevant here: "*old age, in itself, is traumatic for survivors*" (italics in original). Relocating to a new country, being separated from his second wife, becoming increasingly isolated from any social circle, the very threat of mortality which hovers ever closer with advancing age, are all situations which may have reactivated elements of the original trauma in his flight from the Nazis.

In choosing a psychotherapeutic approach, we took into consideration the nature of his defenses. Anshel, as with paranoid psychotics generally, projected internal anxieties onto external situations. *The prospects of an insight-oriented psychodynamic therapy bearing fruit with an aging Holocaust survivor were not favorable* (Krystal, 1981). With the difficulty Anshel experienced regarding basic trust (Chodoff, 1980), a true therapeutic alliance could not be expected to develop. Anshel showed none of the insight necessary for such an undertaking. We were certainly wary of the risks involved in tampering with the defense mechanisms which had allowed him to survive this long.

We attempted to provide for Anshel a *supportive environment* where he would feel as little threatened as possible. In such a setting, Anshel felt sufficiently comfortable to speak about his past and he did so at great length. This served two possible functions. First of all, Anshel's repeated retelling of the dangers which he had faced and survived may have aided him in some small way in his effort to come to terms with the ghosts from his past. Secondly, the value of *reminiscence* as a form of psychotherapy, especially for an elderly population, has been noted (Bachar et al., 1991; Cook, 1991). Reminiscence may contribute to the integration of the ego in the elderly person. As noted, integration is a central task of old age, but one which can elude many Holocaust survivors. Telling of his past may have helped Anshel escape the chasm of despair.

We were certainly aware that there were severe limits to what we could reasonably expect from such therapy. Anshel would not speak of his former, pre-Holocaust life. That seemed to no longer exist for him; it was beyond the realm of his reminiscing. Therefore, he also was not able to mourn. Any self-integration that he achieved was accordingly limited.

To help Anshel fully overcome his internal demons and past trauma was not possible, and not attempted. But with more modest goals, we did succeed in restoring a small semblance of calm to his life.

REFERENCES

American Psychiatric Association (1987). *Diagnostic and statistical manual* (3rd ed.-revised). Washington, DC:Author.

Bachar, E., Kindler, S., Schefler, G., & Lerer, B. (1991). Reminiscing as a technique in the group psychotherapy of depression: A comparative study. *British Journal of Clinical Psychology, 30,* 375-377.

Chodoff, P. (1980). Psychotherapy with the survivor. In J. Dimsdale (Ed.), *Survivors, Victims and Perpetrators* (pp. 205-218). Washington, D.C.: Hemisphere Publishing.

Cook, B. A. (1991). The effects of reminiscence on psychological measures of ego integrity in elderly nursing home residents. *Archives of Psychiatric Nursing, 5,* 292-298.

Danieli, Y. (1981). The aging survivor of the Holocaust: Discussion: On the achievement of integration in aging survivors of the Nazi Holocaust. *Journal of Geriatric Psychiatry, 14,* 191-210.

Erikson, E. H. (1963). *Childhood and society* (2nd ed.). New York: W. W. Norton.

Krystal, H. (1981). The aging survivor of the Holocaust: Integration and self-healing in posttraumatic states. *Journal of Geriatric Psychiatry, 14,* 165-189.

Hypnotherapy and Regulated Uncovering in the Treatment of Older Survivors of Nazi Persecution

Eli Somer, PhD

EDITOR'S INTRODUCTION TO THE CHAPTER: In some ways, the previous case of paranoia also makes a nice contrast with depression. While the paranoids deny that they have a problem (and merely blame others), depressives tend to introject blame and shame from others.

In other ways, dissociative reaction is the opposite of paranoia. The former represses traumatic memories, while the latter indulges in traumatic fantasies and then projects them. If paranoids can be treated without insight, then dissociative reaction may require insight. While paranoids can be treated with supportive therapy, dissociative reaction may require a dramatic process of uncovering. There is no more useful tool in this than hypnotherapy.

I am not certain if the following case of a 58 year old Israeli woman is more depressed or dissociative, but Somer demonstrates the need to prepare the patient for hypnotherapy with appropriate medications as well as with psychotherapy. Furthermore, after the abreaction, the patient must receive additional treatment to deal with uncovered grief.

The debate over whether it is necessary and wise to uncover painful memories in the aged is not resolved, and will continue in this forum. However, if such uncovery is to take place, we should

Eli Somer is affiliated with the R. D. Wolfe Centre for Study of Psychological Stress, University of Haifa, Haifa 31999, Israel.

[Haworth co-indexing entry note]: "Hypnotherapy and Regulated Uncovering in the Treatment of Older Survivors of Nazi Persecution." Somer, Eli. Co-published simultaneously in the *Clinical Gerontologist* (The Haworth Press, Inc.) Vol. 14, No. 3, 1994, pp. 47-65; and: *Holocaust Survivors' Mental Health* (ed: T. L. Brink) The Haworth Press, Inc., 1994, pp. 47-65. Multiple copies of this article/chapter may be purchased from The Haworth Document Delivery Center [1-800-3-HAWORTH; 9:00 a.m. - 5:00 p.m. (EST)].

47

follow Somer's guidelines in order to minimize risks to the patient and secure maximum therapeutic outcome.

Survivors of the Nazi Holocaust have continued to suffer from depression, sleep disturbances, nightmares, chronic anxiety and a variety of somatic problems. Psychotherapeutic work with the survivors has been relatively ineffective primarily because some of these posttraumatic patients were unable to access their harmful experiences. Denial, repression and dissociation are among the commonly employed defense mechanisms that prevent adequate processing and subsequent integration of their atrocious pasts. The treatment of chronic and complicated post-traumatic-stress-disorder (PTSD) is a challenging and demanding undertaking for both patient and therapist and frequently requires emotionally strenuous uncovering. The now aging Holocaust survivors may be put at risk if affectively intense abreactive treatments are employed. This chapter concerns itself with advisable precautions to be implemented if uncovering of repressed material with these often medically compromised patients is indicated. A gradual regulated hypnotherapeutic approach that safeguards the older patient from undue stress is described.

The psychological aftermath of Nazi persecution on Holocaust survivors has been studied and documented throughout the last half of the century (Chodoff, 1980, Eitinger and Strom, 1973, Eitinger, 1980, Hoppe, 1971, Niederland, 1964). Survivors who availed themselves of psychotherapy seemed to have continued to suffer from depression, a variety of somatic and pain disorders, sleep and dream disturbances and pervasive anxiety (Eitinger, 1980), as well as from personality disorders associated with chronic aggression (Hoppe, 1971), failed empathy (Laub & Auerhahn, 1989), anhedonia and alexithymia (Krystal, 1978a, 1978b). Fifty years after World War II survivors need to adjust to the challenges of senescence as they continue to struggle with the debilitating effects of their harmful past experiences. The last phases of human development associated with old age involve the need to revise and evaluate one's life. With a diminishing future one is left with the challenge of renunciation. The need is to compare one's past life goals and aspirations with outcomes and achievements, to redefine one's being through the having been, to give meaning to past arbitrary inevitabilities, to accept failures and lost opportunities and to integrate embedded memories into peaceful acceptance. Retirement and aging frequently are associated with diminishing gratification, increased somatic discomfort, gradual loss of autonomy and the need to cope with death of friends and loved ones. These stressors can reactivate repressed past traumata and produce extraordinary psychological pain. Before I examine the special considerations in hypnotherapy with aged survivors of the Holocaust let me review some known outcomes of catastrophic psychic trauma.

EMOTIONAL EFFECTS
OF THE HOLOCAUST EXPERIENCE

The surrender to the unavoidable danger, rather than the exposure to intense overwhelming stimuli, is the key variable in adult catastrophic trauma (Krystal, 1971). The process of learned helplessness often led to automatic obedience through blocking of affective and pain reactions. The process has been termed by Lifton (1967) as a "psychic closing off." This emotional anaesthetic, a dissociative defence mechanism, was adaptive for survival in the concentration camps. The process, however, frequently has lasted long after the liberation, resulting in a continuation of cognitive constriction, helplessness, non-assertiveness and passivity. A perpetuation of the traumatic process is manifested in nightmares depicting a dreaded calamity, hypervigilance, expectational anxiety and displaced screen phobias related to threatening memories.

Another rarely resolved theme in the lives of survivors is related to what Primo Levi (1961), described as the experience of being "desperately and ferociously alone" (p. 80). The essence of the Holocaust experience is not only the inability to affect the interpersonal environment, but also what Laub and Auerhahn (1989) described as a massive failure of the interpersonal environment to mediate both basic physical needs as well as needs for empathy. The Nazis not only killed Jews but also managed first to destroy their victims' self image as humans. So radical and brutal was the Nazi negation of Jews that it severely debilitated their sense of mutuality, their hopes to be heard and their capacity to be aware of theirselves.

This handicap helps survivors to avoid the overwhelming emotional burden associated with their memories.

According to the Dutch psychiatrist Bastiaans (1974), the survivors' capacity for control and repression eventually diminishes, possibly because of early aging symptoms they tend to develop as a result of the physical hardships of the camp (Eitinger, 1964). Israeli studies concerning adjustment of survivors found that they are more vulnerable to the stresses of life, they are more depressed and less optimistic (Dor-Shav, 1975). Others conclude that the chronic concentration camp syndrome has not been very responsive to psychotherapy (Dasberg, 1987, Krystal, 1991).

PSYCHOTHERAPEUTIC ISSUES IN THE TREATMENT OF SURVIVORS

Obstacles

One major inherent problem hinders the psychotherapeutic process with survivor patients. In response to the overwhelming experiences, victims have failed to master their vehement depression, anxiety and anger. They fragmented the experience and repressed its threatening components. Frequently, only traces of the original trauma avail themselves to conscious awareness. The ensuing affective, cognitive, behavioral and somatic disturbances associated with the intense unresolved experience become isolated and clinically unyielding symptoms. The resolution of the traumatic experience is rendered impossible because it is greatly unintegrated and therefore, frequently, unrecognized. If the narrative of the trauma with all its integrated experiencial modalities is unavailable to the patient, interpretative work would be futile.

In psychodynamic terms, severe trauma creates primary repression in which no trace of a registration of any kind is left in the psyche (Kingston and Cohen, 1986). While psychodynamic theory of coping with trauma deals with repression in relationship with internal personality functioning and unresolved early conflicts (Kardiner, 1941; Fenichel, 1945), Janet proposed dissociation and the idea of vertical splits in personality that bring about new cores of consciousness that store parts of the threatening experience, safely isolating them from conscious awareness (Van der Hart and Friedman, 1989). Thus, when a split exists between ego states, there is no guarantee that psychotherapeutic work done with one ego state will permeate to the others and affect them. Most survivors described at least moderate degrees of depersonalization and derealization upon exposure to the unbelievable reality of the Nazi terror (Bettelheim, 1960; Blum, 1948; Cohen, 1953; Levi, 1961). I suggest that severely and chronically traumatized victims have continued to use these once adaptive survival mechanisms. These processes later evolved into rigid dissociative defenses that prevent adequate healing in conventional psychotherapy.

Overcoming Dissociation

Back in the early 1960s a few reports started to recognize the need to help some of the psychotherapeutically resistant survivors to relive their experiences. While Engel (1962), for example, believed such processes would also help "long repressed affects of defiance and counter-aggression" (p. 202), he advocated Narcoanalytic and hypnotic methods to help those patients resolve their traumatic experiences. Niederland (1964) advocated that the only way to help the psychologically debilitated survivors was to take them back in time and have them work through, against their enormous resistance, the traumatizing events. Although he had failed to specify the techniques he recommended to be used, Niederland did propose to "use the charged hypermnestic material appearing in their dreams and nightmares to overcome gaps of memory . . . and to arrive via association and detailed exploration of the persecution events at the deeper layers of guilt, shame and fear connected with these experiences" (p. 473).

Hypnosis has been considered a method of choice in the treatment of dissociative disorders (Kingsbury, 1988). It is a process which actually facilitates dissociation between different cognitive systems and between physical and emotional sensations (Hilgard, 1970). The perspective of hypnosis as controlled dissociation renders it a useful tool in psychotherapy for posttraumatic disorders (Spiegel & Cardena, 1990). There has been a renewed and growing interest in both the role of dissociation in various psychiatric disorders, as well as in the potential contribution of hypnosis in the treatment of these problems. One of the principles emerging from the study of the now more readily identified dissociative reactions is that, indeed, the vast majority of those disorders are traumatically induced (Putnam, 1985). When one systematically inquires about such experiences, dissociative phenomena such as out-of-body experiences, amnesia and profound detachment are commonly described by combat veterans (Ewalt & Crawford, 1981). Strong evidence exists today, linking the development of the most extreme pathology of dissociation–multiple personality disorder (MPD) to severe, recurrent traumatic experiences usually occurring during childhood or early adolescence (Putnam, 1989). Several authors have suggested that similar processes and outcomes have been developed by survivors of sustained life-threatening experiences, such as internment in a concentration camp (Frankenthal, 1969, Bettelheim, 1979). The etiological and clinical similarities that exist between survivors of Nazi persecution and survivors of prolonged child abuse enable us to borrow from the considerable MPD treatment experience accumulated thus far. An extensive discussion of the treatment of MPD and dissociative disorders available elsewhere (Braun, 1986; Putnam, 1989), is beyond scope of this article. The critical issue for this paper is that severe dissociative disorders though treatable, present for both patient and therapist an arduous task that almost involves strong affective experiences, vigorous abreactions and prolonged exposures to deeply unsettling and upsetting materials (Kluft, 1984).

Can the aging and often physically compromised survivors of the Nazi Holocaust withstand such an undertaking or will the methods that proved successful with less vulnerable younger survivors of prolonged traumata actually endanger our older patients?

Hypnoanalytic Techniques

Hypnotic abreaction has a long history. Janet (1925) Pioneered it in the 1870s, Freud and Breuer utilized it in the 1880s for the treatment of hysteria (1955). Abreaction assumes an hydraulic model of the personality. According to this model posttraumatic symptoms are a consequence of repressed emotions. The goal of treatment is the recovery of amnestic material to facilitate free expression of pent-up emotions, to reconstruct memory and integrate the experience.

In his work with older survivors the therapist must give supreme priority to *the first rule of Hippocrates: First do not harm*. Treatment needs to employ progressive uncovering, working through and integration which enable the patient to gain a sense of cognitive and emotional control over the threatening repressed traumata, as well as adequate protection against retraumatization (Brende & Benedict, 1980; Spiegel, 1981).

In his work with older MPD patients, Kluft (1988) insists on the patients having a personal physician with whom he could discuss the medical aspects of their capacity to tolerate extreme stress. Cardiovascular stress tests and 24-hour electrocardiogram monitoring are among the recommended preliminary diagnostic evaluations to be taken. To assess the patients' capacities for the uncovering, positive, symptom relief oriented hypnotic experiences are used first. This process enhances trust and bonding with the therapist. It also contributes to an optimistic expectation as far as treatment efficacy is concerned.

Survivors are sometimes able to ward off intrusion of traumatic experience into consciousness by suppressing hypnotic ability. Brown and Fromm (1986) have observed that posttraumatic stress disorder (PTSD) patients can initially appear to be poorly hypnotizable and quite agitated during induction. To avoid sudden emergence of intense affect or traumatic re-enactment they suggest to delay the use of hypnosis in favor of waking relaxing imagery and parallel interpretation of the resistance to hypnosis as possible posttraumatic defensive symptomatology. The chronic exposure to dehumanizing life-threatening circumstances had impaired normal affective development of many young victims and had precipitated a pathological formation of identity. Nevertheless, these patients seldom associate their psychological deficiencies and distress with the experience of their horrific past.

I frequently try to educate the patients about the nature of their problem and it's inevitable relationship with the difficult events of the war. Open discussion of the typical psychological manifestations of PTSD normalizes their abnormality. That is, it defines their symptoms as a normal reaction to an abnormal situation. This can not only further enhance the therapeutic bond but it also conveys messages of recognition and respect to a degraded pathological self-representation often found among Holocaust survivors (Krystal, 1968). Horowitz (1973) asserted that a psycho-educational component in therapy can facilitate better cooperation with the cognitive/affective processing of the trauma, necessary for recovery. If the patients are sufficiently educated and are not afflicted with any psychiatric organicity, I also tend to encourage them to read historical material concerning their plight, as well as literature on PTSD and the survivor syndrome. This could not only be a first waking state step in accessing repressed material, but it also provides a conceptual framework for their condition. During this first stabilization phase I attempt to determine the patients' capacity to utilize relaxation skills and ego-strengthening suggestions. I also try to evaluate their ability to reduce distress in the subsequent uncovering.

Based on these assessments I decide whether or not to move on. I next tend to utilize an intervention Bellak and Faithem (1981) termed "mediate catharsis." In this technique, also used by Kluft (1988) for the treatment of older survivors of incest, I guide the patients in waking imagery to known or suspected emotionally charged situations of the past for which the patient has either no specified recollection or no access to affect. To this guided imagery I add an emotional "soundtrack" by expressing the affect I suspect the patient felt. This process bypasses alexithymic numbing and may facilitate enrichment of the psychological experience. Another technique I use to help the patient associate the various components of the dissociated trauma experience is the "affect bridge" (Watkins, 1971). This method can only be utilized if any particular feeling is salient and is experienced with some intensity. It is of particular usefulness with patients who display dissociated and unyielding affective symptoms. The technique could be first tried with positive feelings such as happiness, but with anhedonic patients, sadness, anger or fear are frequently the only available emotions. The patient is asked to imagine that he is travelling along a bridge of emotion to a time earlier in his life when he felt exactly the same. This second phase of therapy gently attempts to perforate the anaesthetic repressive and amnestic barriers of the survivor.

Hypnoprojective methods can also be used in the service of a preliminary uncovering approach. The "Cloud Fantasy," "Crystal Gazing," or the "Theatre Technique" (Brown & Fromm, 1986) are alternative ways of allowing the survivors' unconscious mind to project scenes that are safely disguised yet cautiously revealing. To be able to proceed without risking maladaptive anxiety or depression states, one must be ready to help the patient enhance tolerance for the emerging or intensifying feelings. One of my favorite methods for attenuating affect in survivors is the "Safe Place" method, in which it is suggested that upon having given a signal the patient will find himself in a very comfortable and safe place. The patient is then asked to describe the safe place and is reminded that he can return to it whenever he fears overwhelming emotions begin to come up. Encouraging the survivors to apply auto-relaxation and self-soothing methods is not only a relevant adjunct technique but also an important curative approach facilitating the symbolic formation of a healthier self-representation capable of internal empathy and nurturance.

A suggested means of controlling the abreactive phase is to have survivors utilize their own defenses as affect regulating mechanisms. The therapist can suggest that the patients operate an imaginary videotape via a remote control device that can both turn the channels as well as control the brightness and volume of the picture on the monitor. The dissociation of the experiencing ego (projected on the monitor) from the observing ego enables the elderly patient to modify the intensity of the emotional experience to tolerable levels.

Another variation on this idea is the "slow-leak" technique (Kluft, 1988). The therapist can suggest to the hypnotized patient that their toxic feelings and impressions cannot be contained forever and thus should be deliberately allowed to leak in minuscule droplets at a rate that would provide no risk to the survivor.

A third recommended precautionary technique to dilute the intensity of affect is to do frequent "fractionated abreactions" (Fine, 1991) rather then a full abreaction. This method helps the patient uncover the encapsulated trauma in small increments. In a desensitizing manner, feelings are slowly reconnected to discrete aspects of the newly uncovered history of the survivor.

Finally, it is advised that each session in which hypnotic uncovering is achieved should be closed with a suggestion for posthypnotic amnesia. Such a message should suggest that the patient will remember only what he is ready to remember and that he will gradually come to reown all the events, feelings and meanings necessary for his healing.

ILLUSTRATIVE CASE STUDY

Background

Bronya is an Israeli woman, Holocaust survivor born in Poland. She was 58 years old at the time of therapy. She has a son, a married daughter and three grandchildren. Bronya has a Master's degree in social-work, which she earned in her mid-fifties. Because she is married to an independently wealthy lawyer, she has preferred to volunteer her time, working on behalf of Jewish Ethiopian immigrants. She has performed this job as if it were a duty, appearing to be rather detached and intellectualizing with regard to her motives. Bronya, the sole survivor of her family, arrived in Israel in 1949 with a group of orphaned young survivors and was put up in a boarding school. She was one of the very few children who had survived Auschwitz. The patient was self-referred for hypnoanalysis and treatment of onset insomnia, fear of the dark, recurrent depressive symptoms and frequent episodes of explosive anger. Additionally, the patient suffered from high blood-pressure, irritable bowel syndrome, chronic headaches and arthritis. Two years prior to the beginning of this psychotherapy, the patient had suffered a mild myocardial infarction. She had been treated with beta-blockers and analgesics.

Although Bronya had some circumstantial explanations for her labile moods, she considered them to be both excessive and damaging. Previously, she had been in therapy with two psychoanalytically oriented psychotherapists, who helped her to better understand the relationship between her current anxiety and anger, and her experiences during World War II. Nevertheless, Bronya noticed only a slight change in the severity of her symptoms. After almost a year without psychotherapy, she decided to seek help again. Her last crisis followed an intensive anxiety reaction she suffered as a result of a traffic ticket given to her on Holocaust Memorial Day.

Bronya was eleven years old when she saw the American liberators enter the gates of Auschwitz. This ended a one year internment in the death camp, where her parents were annihilated. The patient's life was saved in Auschwitz by a non-Jewish female physician who adopted the child and had employed her in the camp's infirmary.

Medical Preparation

Bronya's physician was consulted with regard to her capacity to withstand the potential stress which traumatic repressed material might elicit if tapped. He encouraged us to proceed with hypnoanalysis, but advised against sudden exposures to extreme emotional arousal. The physician decided to prophylactically increase the dosage of her beta-blockers. Doses of Propranolol were raised to 240 mg per day, which was given in 3 equal daily doses. As an additional protective measure, she was also put on 75 mg per day of Oxazepan, a benzodiazepine, also administered in divided doses. For the duration of the hypnoanalytic intervention the patient was scheduled for weekly blood-pressure monitoring appointments with the clinic's nurse.

Initial Assessment Phase

During the first five sessions, the patient's life history was taken. She also completed the Hebrew version of the MMPI (Montag, 1977) and the Dissociative Experience Scale (DES) (Bernstein and Putnam, 1986). The diagnostic impression was one of post-traumatic-stress-disorder, chronic; with dissociative features and psychosomatic correlates. The patient was amnestic to almost the entire duration of her imprisonment in Auschwitz.

Fragmentary recall was devoid of any affect. The patient had only scarce memories of the years prior to her internment in the death camp. She felt as if her life began only following her liberation and subsequent immigration to Israel.

Bronya was interested in trying hypnoanalysis and hypnotherapy in the hope of relieving what seemed to her as life-long suffering.

Psychological Preparation

In order to enhance bonding with the hypnotherapist, to assess Bronya's hypnotic abilities and to help her build both a sense of inner-safety and self-mastery, she was first taught autorelaxation and a few pain management skills to help her gain initial symptom relief. The patient demonstrated a capability to utilize imagery and cognitive-behavioral skills, and seemed to be encouraged by her newly discovered self-efficacy. She was later taught to create a mental "safe place" and was given practice in both accessing it, as well as enjoying herself in it. Her chosen image was one of drinking ice-coffee in a jacuzzi hot tub.

Initial Exploration

In our fifth psychotherapy session I started taking a very detailed history of the patient's life. She was the only child of a working class, religiously observant father and a protective, demanding, but warm mother, who had been a homemaker. Bronya was only five years old when the Germans invaded Poland and terminated her normal childhood. The patient was never sure whether her scant memories were products of her dreams and imagination or, rather, traces of her past reality. Her description of the persecutions, the deportations and the losses she endured, were vague and emotionally empty. Initial attempts to access the patient's affect was through a guided waking imagery, to which the patient had to imagine not only the described sights and sounds, but also the correspondent emotions.

For example: "You are getting ready to leave your home in Warsaw. You do not, really, know what is going on, but Mom and Dad seem, to be really worried. They tell you, you will all be coming back, but you can tell Mother is very upset. You are worried and scared. You don't want to go downstairs where the soldiers are angrily shouting words in a language you do not understand . . ."

Bronya responded well to such exploratory "emotional sound-tracing." Major known events from her childhood were fed-back to her in that fashion. The patient reported in the subsequent debriefings that although she could occasionally sympathize with the imagined "Bronya the girl," and feel sad for her, she had been observing these described events as an outside onlooker. She was obviously still dissociating from many of the related feelings. Interestingly, the patient had started reporting at that time a correspondent deterioration in her initial presenting symptoms, and expressed concern over the potential danger of this therapy. She was consequently given further explanations regarding the nature and treatment of post-traumatic dissociation. Bronya was also reinforced for her courage and was reassured that she was, indeed, making progress.

Abreactive Exploration

The utilization of hypnoanalytic techniques started on our 19th session. Bronya came in visibly upset. She reported bitter quarrels with her husband and inexplicable, intense anxiety that worsened at night. The symptomatic episode had apparently started a few hours after the following incident: in her line of duty as a volunteer social worker, she found herself helping a crying girl who was being separated from her father as he was being arrested for domestic violence.

Bronya was able to make the obvious rational connections between this incident and its emotional ramifications, and her own past. However, no associated traumatic memories were recalled. To lessen some of the anticipated affect, Bronya was asked first to go to her "safe place" and to relax in her imaginary hot tub. She had also been reminded that at any point in her hypnoanalysis, she might be given the suggestion to go to her "safe place" and that she would be able to follow the suggestion with complete enthrallment and relaxation. The patient was then put in a hypnotic trance and was asked to imagine a bridge of anger and fear, that began at the arrest scene she had recently witnessed, and spanned all the way to an earlier time when she had had similar emotions. She was then encouraged to walk on that bridge to its other end. As expected, Bronya found Auschwitz on the other side. She was in her father's arms, her mother standing close by. They had just got off the train.

Guards were shouting, and their German Shepherds were barking viciously. A tall officer asked her parents some questions. Then her father had to go to a different line. The child cried for her father. Tears were rolling down Bronya's face as she was describing the last time she saw her father, her body started to tremor with anxiety. At that point, she was promptly asked to go back to her "safe place" and relax. Out of trance, we later discussed the relationship between the precipitating trigger event, her intense emotional reactions, and the original trauma.

In the following months, Bronya was seen twice a week. She started to share very rich dream material, that when elaborated and explored in hypnoanalysis with the "videotape technique," provided a wealth of repressed memories associated with scenes of witnessed Nazi cruelty, loneliness and fear.

Post Abreactive Psychotherapy

In the next phases of therapy, Bronya was supported through a period of genuine grief she had experienced over her murdered parents and her lost childhood. She was only later able to recognize the fear she had of expressing anger toward the Nazis. The rage against the perpetrators had been, eventually, accessed and re-owned. The angry feelings were so intense, they had to be first released in an attenuated way, in a fractionated abreaction under hypnosis. In some of these sessions, the patient imagined herself returning to Auschwitz with the Israel Defence Forces, liberating the camp's inmates and bringing "little Bronya" back home with them to Israel.

The last phases of therapy focused on resolving Bronya's guilt over the pain and distress she had caused to her current family throughout the years. The treatment was terminated with several family therapy sessions, in which she shared with her loved ones, for the first time, the now accessable emotional testimony of her ordeals during the Holocaust.

Epilogue

Eighteen months after this treatment started, Bronya felt she was ready to terminate it. Although she was still uneasy in the dark and continued to avoid being alone at night, she was much calmer and considerably less angry. Physically, there was little improvement in her high blood-pressure. However, it seemed to be controlled with medication. Improvements were reported with regard to the frequency and intensity of her chronic headaches. Her irritable bowel symptoms appeared to have gone completely and at the end of therapy Bronya no longer suffered from sleep disturbance. However, years of marital conflict have taken their toll on the marriage. Her husband was emotionally alienated and showed no more sexual attraction to her. Even though the couple was uninterested in further marital therapy, they did continue to be committed to each other.

On a follow-up telephone interview, conducted half a year after the treatment had ended, Bronya reported she was still maintaining her gains. She also told me that her husband and she had just returned from a trip to Poland. Bronya had fulfilled an old wish to lay flowers in the gas chamber and near the ovens where her parents perished.

DISCUSSION

Krystal (1991) has argued that psychotherapeutic work with Holocaust survivors has been ineffective because they fear their emotions and because they suffer from profound repression which prevents recognition of their inner reality.

Uncovering and abreactions are necessary components in the treatment of survivors of prolonged traumatic stress. Their purpose is to educate, to achieve continuity of memory content and to release encapsulated traumatic affect.

Hypnosis can be a valuable tool in attaining these goals. Other survivors who have not fully benefited from past therapies, may gain from therapeutically active progressive attempts to recover, work through and reincorporate traumata of the past. Hypnosis can help the patient gain a sense of control over the potentially intrusive experiences, and thus, makes them more available for psychotherapeutic processing. The utilization of hypnosis can also provide the survivor with the emotionally corrective experience of the therapist's solidarity and empathy. The hypnotherapist who works with the complicated Holocaust PTSD patient must function as a benevolent self-object (Kohut, 1971), showing active care and support.

Time is running out on the now aging and rapidly dying survivors. Many of them have learned to tolerate high levels of distress and a compromised quality of life. The sense of haste is indeed sometimes ours, the therapists'. Allowing these victims to carry their testimony buried in their wounded souls and ailing bodies could, to my mind, amount to a symbolic victory for the perpetrators. The sense of obligation we feel towards these elderly survivors should, however, never be translated into pressure to engage in emotionally strenuous uncovering procedures. Patients are definitely to be encouraged to participate in the setting of their therapy goals but sometimes we need to over-rule ambitious strivings for any hypothetically ideal outcome in favour of concerns for the patients' safety. A cognitive behavioral model is a viable alternative for survivors who cannot engage in uncovering but may need to learn how to modify maladaptive cognitions, acquire assertiveness skills or learn voluntary control of autonomic hyperactivity. The therapeutic suggestions provided in this paper should be implemented with caution and regarded as preliminary. Unfortunately, systematic outcome research of hypnotherapeutic uncovering with Holocaust survivors has yet to be carried out. It is hoped that this paper will promote further interest in this area and that, subsequently, we will soon acquire a better knowledge concerning the best curative approaches for these surviving victims.

REFERENCES

Bastiaans, J. (1979). Het KZ-syndroom en de menselijke vrjheid. *Nederlands Tijdschrift voor Geneeskunde, 118*, 1173-1178.

Bellak, L. & Faithorn, P. (1981). *Crises and special problems in psychoanalysis and psychotherapy.* New York: Brunner/Mazel.

Bernstein. E.M. & Putnam, F.W. (1986). Development, Reliability, and Validity of a Dissociation Scale. *Journal of Nervous and Mental Disease, 174,* 727-735.

Bettelheim, B. (1960). *The informed heart.* Glencoe, Illinois: Free Press.

Bettelheim, B. (1979). *Surviving and other essays.* New York: Harcourt Brace Jovanovich.

Bluhm, H.O. (1948). How did they survive? *American Journal of Psychotherapy, 2,* 1-9.

Braun, B.G. (ed.) (1986). *Treatment of multiple personality disorder.* Washington, DC: American Psychiatric Press.

Brende, J.O. & Benedict, B.O. (1980). The Vietnam combat delayed stress syndrome: Hypnotherapy of "dissociative symptoms." *American Journal of Clinical Hypnosis, 23,* 34-40.

Breuer, J. & Freud, S. (1955). Studies of hysteria. I: On physical mechanisms of hysterical phenomena: preliminary communication. In: J. Strachey (ed.), *Standard Edition, 2,* pp. 1-181. London: Hogarth Press (original work published 1893-95).

Brown, D.P. & Fromm, E. (1988). *Hypnotherapy and hypnoanalysis.* Hillsdale, New Jersey: Lawrence Erlbaum Associates, Publishers.

Chodoff, P. (1980). Psychotherapy with the survivor. In: Dinsdale, J. (ed.). *Survivors, victims and perpetrators.* Washington: Hemisphere Publishers.

Cohen, E.A. (1953). *Human behavior in the concentration camp.* New York: Norton.

Dasberg, H. (1987). Psychological distress of Holocaust survivors and offspring in Israel, forty years later: A review. *Israel Journal of Psychiatry and Related Sciences, 24,* 243.-256.

Dor-Shav, N.K. (1978). On the long-range effects of concentration camp internment on Nazi victims: 25 years later. *Journal of Consulting and Clinical Psychology, 46,* 1-11.

Eitinger, L. (1964). *Concentration camps survivors in Norway and Israel.* Oslo/London: Oslo Universitets forbaget/Allen and Unwin.

Eitinger, L. & Strom, A. (1973). *Mortality and morbidity of excessive stress.* New York: Jason Aronson.

Eitinger, L. (1980). The concentration camp syndrome and its late sequence. In: Dimsdale, J. (ed.). *Survivors, victims and perpetrators.* Washington: Hemisphere Publishers.

Engel, W.H. (1962). Reflections on the psychiatric consequences of persecution. *American Journal of Psychotherapy, 16,* 191-203.

Erickson, E.H. (1963). *Childhood and society (2nd ed.).* New York: Norton.

Erwalt, J.R. & Crawford, D. (1981). Posttraumatic stress syndrome. *Current Psychiatric Therapy, 20,* 145-153.

Fenichel, P. (1945). *The psychoanalytic theory of neurosis.* New York: Norton.

Fine, C.G. (1991). Treatment stabilization and crisis prevention: pacing the therapy of the multiple personality disorder patient. *Psychiatric Clinics of North America, 14,* 661-675.

Frankenthal, K. (1969). Autohypnosis and other aids for survival in situations of extreme stress. *International Journal of Clinical and Experimental Hypnosis, 17,* 153-159.

Hilgard, J.R. (1970). *Personality and hypnosis: A study of imaginative involvement.* Chicago: The University of Chicago Press.

Hoppe, K.D. (1971a). The aftermath of Nazi persecution reflected in recent psychiatric literature. *International Psychiatry Clinics, 8,* 169-198.

Hoppe, K.D. (1971b). Chronic reactive aggression in survivors of severe persecution. *Comprehensive Psychiatry, 12,* 230-236.

Horowitz, M.J. (1973). Phase oriented treatment of stress response syndromes. *American Journal of Psychotherapy, 27,* 506-515.

Janet, P. (1925). *Psychological healing: a historical and clinical study* (Eden Paul & Cedar Paul, Trans.). New York: McMillan (originally published 1919).

Kardiner, A. (1941). *The Traumatic Neurosis of War.* New York: Paul Hoeber.

Kingsbury, S.J. (1988). Hypnosis in the treatment of posttraumatic stress disorder. An isomorphic intervention. *American Journal of Clinical Hypnosis, 31,* 81-90.

Kingston, W., Cohen, J. (1986). Primal repression: clinical and theoretical aspects. *International Journal of Psychoanalysis, 67,* 337-356.

Kluft, R.P. (1984). Aspects of the treatment of multiple personality disorder. *Psychiatric annals, 14,* 51-55.

Kluft, R.P. (1988). On treating the older patient with multiple personality disorder: "Race against time," or "Make haste slowly?" *American Journal of Clinical Hypnosis, 30,* 257-267.

Kohut, H. (1971). *The analysis of the self.* New York: International Universities Press.

Krystal, H. (ed.) (1968). *Massive psychic trauma.* New York: International Universities Press.

Krystal, H. (1971): Trauma: consideration of severity and chronicity. In: H. Krystal and W. Niederland (eds.), *Psychic Traumatization.* Boston: Little, Brown & Co.

Krystal, H. (1978a). Trauma and affects. *Psychoanalytic Study of the Child, 33,* 81-116.

Krystal, H. (1978b). Self representation and the capacity for self-care. In: *The Annual of Psychoanalysis, VI,* 209-246.

Krystal, H. (1991). Integration and self-healing in posttraumatic states: A ten year retrospective. *American Imago, 48,* 93-118.

Laub, D. & Auerhahn, N.C. (1989). Failed empathy–a central theme in the survivors' Holocaust experience. *Psychoanalytic Psychology, 6,* 377-400.

Levi, P. (1961). *Survival in Auschwitz.* New York: Collier.

Lifton, R.J. (1967). *Death in life: Survivors of Hiroshima.* New York: Random House.

Montag, I. *The Tel-Aviv MMPI: Some Validation Studies.* Paper presented at the University of Haifa symposium on personality tests, Haifa, May 1977.

Niederland, W. (1967). Psychiatric disorders among persecution victims. *Journal of Mental and Nervous Diseases, 139,* 450-476.

Putnam. F.W. (1985). Dissociation as a response to extreme trauma. In Kluft, R.P. (Ed.). *The childhood antecedents of multiple personality.* Washington, DC: American Psychiatric Press.

Putnam. F.W. (1989). *Diagnosis and treatment of multiple personality disorder.* New York: The Guilford Press.

Spiegel, D. (1981). Vietnam grief work using hypnosis. *American Journal of Clinical Hypnosis, 23*, 239-247.

Spiegel, D. & Cardena, E. (1990). New uses of hypnosis in the treatment of posttraumatic stress disorder. *Journal of Clinical Psychiatry, 51*, 39-43.

Van der Hart, O. & Friedman, B. (1989). A reader's guide to Pierre Janet on dissociation: a neglected intellectual heritage. *Dissociation, 2*, 3-16.

Watkings, J.G. (1971). The affect bridge: A hypnoanalytic technique. *International Journal of Abnormal and Social Psychology, 42*, 256-259.

Forgetting Childhood:
A Defense Mechanism Against Psychosis
in a Holocaust Survivor

Ilan Modai, MD

EDITOR'S INTRODUCTION TO THE CHAPTER: On with the debate about uncovering painful memories of the Holocaust. Modai's case is remarkably similar to the previous one. The patient is a 58 year old woman who is similarly unable to remember her childhood. She also suffers from problems in interpersonal relations and has an unstable mood (although probably not full-blown manic-depression). Modai concludes that the dissociation in these cases is a defense which is best not removed. Rather, it is preferable to use empathy and transferential work to strengthen basic trust.

INTRODUCTION

Holocaust survivors experienced such hardships that human imagination can not tolerate. Non-psychiatric survivors manifest more health complaints, are more anhedonic and pessimistic, are more anxious in the face of additional stress, show more cognitive restrictions, have more rigid psychological defenses and are ha-

Ilan Modai is Head of Department h' at the Gehah Psychiatric Hospital, and Senior Lecturer at the Sackler Faculty of Medicine, Tel Aviv University.

Address correspondence to: Dr. I Modai, Gehah Psychiatric Hospital, P.O. Box 102, Petah Tiqva, Israel.

[Haworth co-indexing entry note]: "Forgetting Childhood: A Defense Mechanism Against Psychosis in a Holocaust Survivor." Modai, Ilan. Co-published simultaneously in the *Clinical Gerontologist* (The Haworth Press, Inc.) Vol. 14, No. 3, 1994, pp. 67-71; and: *Holocaust Survivors' Mental Health* (ed: T. L. Brink) The Haworth Press, Inc., 1994, pp. 67-71. Multiple copies of this article/chapter may be purchased from The Haworth Document Delivery Center [1-800-3-HAWORTH; 9:00 a.m. - 5:00 p.m. (EST)].

bitual *deniers* (Dasberg, 1991). Today, there is a "conspiracy of silence" serving paradoxically both sides, the survivors' shame and the persecutors' need for denial (Dasberg, 1991).

Many survivors have suffered mental and physical breakdowns from the many years of stress. The second generation continue to play the "conspiracy of silence" game. They are shameful about the degradation of the past, feel obliged to compensate for the dead and suffer from separation anxiety (Dasberg, 1987; Davidson, 1981). In psychiatric cases, survivors have guilt feelings of staying alive, suffer from repetitive nightmares, are more susceptible to depressions and manifest paranoidal traits (Niederland, 1961; Klein et al, 1963; Davidson, 1981). Despite the silence kept by some survivors, they never forget what happened.

We present an atypical case of a Holocaust survivor who reacted with total amnesia.

A CASE REPORT

Five years ago, O.K., a fifty eight year-old woman sought help for depression. She suffered from inability to function, low self esteem, lack of concentration, insomnia, suicidal ideations, withdrawal and guilt feelings. She mainly worried about her inability to dance. From adolescence, dancing was her main expression and interpersonal communication. In the first stages of treatment she received clomipramine up to 150 mg/day and a month later when a manic episode emerged, clomipramine was replaced by lithium 600 mg/day. Her mother, also a Holocaust survivor, has been suffering from post Holocaust recurrent depressions without manic episodes. O.K. heard some details about her childhood from a cousin in Israel who witnessed her childhood hardships.

She was born in Hungary, an only child to a Jewish couple of low socioeconomic level. Her father was a minor salesman and her mother was a housewife. When she was eight years old, the Germans first took her father, then a few months later, arrested her mother. She was left with her grandmother who died a few days afterwards. The neighbours found her sitting by her dead grandmother and put her in a monastery. There, she learned to serve Christianity. After the war, she was collected by her parents who survived concentration camps, and sent to a Jewish religious school. When she was 14 years old, she immigrated to Israel with her parents. The immigration ship was arrested by the British authorities and all immigrants were taken to a camp in Cyprus. While getting off the ship, she lost her parents and was found by a British soldier. In Israel she was put in a kibbutz while her parents lived in the city. She visited them once in while during weekends and lived with foster parents in the kibbutz. As a teenager, she was withdrawn and sensitive. She learned to dance and it became the main motive in her life. She also liked to write poems. In these poems she expressed motives relating to the dichotomies between good and evil and despair and hope and expressed also longing for love and affection. All evil symbols were those of nazis, black colour and death. Hope was associated with nature powers such as the sun and the sea. She was shameful of herself and her parents who looked and behaved differently from the born Israelies. Her parents were withdrawn, detached from their surroundings, silent about the past, talked a foreign language and were very rigid. On the other hand, the Israelies represented freedom, self-confidence and power. She served the army and was married twice. During both marriages, she felt restrained, dependent, afraid of intimacy and of losing her freedom. She was detached from her husbands and her two children. In addition, she suffered from vaginismus which improved later on. Once in a while she unwillingly visited her mother who had been hospitalized due to recurrent depressions. The reminiscence of these visits caused arousal of anxiety. She kept on visiting her mother in order to compensate their expectations and reduce her guilt feelings. She was divorced by her first husband and a few years later remarried without love, but because of her need for protection. From age 48 on, she suffered from late bipolar mood disorder, and started psychotherapy when she was 53 years old.

During psychotherapy she suffered from total amnesia of her childhood in Hungary and of everything that happened to her during the Holocaust. When talking about it in a theoretical manner, no feelings were aroused. She could only cognitively imagine a sad story of another child going through all these hardships but without actually feeling anything. Also, she did not dream about any event that happened to her during these hard times. The information she received from her cousin did not revive her memory. Childhood was completely dissociated from the course of her life. An attempt to confront her with actual objects from her past, for instance, sending her to visit the immigrant ship, triggered an immediate manic episode followed by a deep depression and a dangerous suicidal attempt. She tried to jump in front of a big truck.

During the process of psychotherapy, through *empathy and continuous tranferential work,* her basic trust was strengthened, she regained some self confidence, could better express herself by words, her interrelations became more intimate and she started to have warm feelings towards her children. Her longing for fatherly love became so strong that she initiated a few intimate relationships with male-friends for the first time in her life

DISCUSSION

O.K. was clinically suffering from bipolar mood disorder and a narcissistic personality disorder. She went through the Holocaust as a child who suffered repetitive abandonments and confronted death very early in life. Her main defenses against these occurrences were detachment and dissociation. She was withdrawn and self absorbed and built her own fantasmatic "good world" as a dissociation from the evil reality. These mechanisms pushed away the frightening reality and helped her to survive in her own imaginative world. In Israel, she indirectly expressed parts of her inner world in poems and dancing. Dancing was the only language in which she could closely express her emotions and communicate with others who represented the new reality. On the one hand she basically needed much love, empathy and affection, but on the other hand she lost her basic trust in human beings and suffered existential anxiety that caused detachment and withdrawal. The need to function (which she successfully maintained) and to stay in touch with the new reality in Israel together with the danger of disintegration, triggered the dissociation of her memory. The threatening reality during childhood which was then perceived from far-away and behind a "curtain," was completely forgotten as a defense against psychosis. It was so strongly dissociated that even in dreams no reminiscence appeared and the attempt to confront her with actual objects from her past resulted in a psychosis. Because of her ambivalent attitudes and sensitivities, she suffered from dysfunction of interpersonal relations. She longed for affection and recognition but on the other hand was afraid of intimacy and dependence. In spite of the progress in psychotherapy, manifested with improvement in interpersonal relations and better touch with reality, she did not regain her memory of childhood. This remained as a psychotic and dissociated world threatening her integrity and better forgotten.

We believe that in these complicated cases of Holocaust survivors, it is better not to expose the amnestic history but rather strengthen the contact with reality.

REFERENCES

Dasberg H: Psychological distress of holocaust survivors and offsprings in Israel, forty years later: A review. Isr J Psychiatry Relat Sci. 24:243-256, 1987.

Dasberg H: Why we were silent–an Israeli psychiatrist speaks to Germans on psychic pain and past persecution. Isr J Psychiatry Relat Sci. 28:29-38, 1991.

Davidson S: Holcaust survivors and their families–clinical and psychotherapeutic experience. Fam Physician, 10: 313-320, 1981.

Klein H, Zellermayer J, Shanan J: Former concentration camp inmates on a psychiatric ward. Arch Gen Psychiatry, 8:334-342, 1963.

Niederland WG: The problem of the survivor. J Hillside Hosp, 10: 233-247, 1961.

SECTION THREE: GROUP AND FAMILY APPROACHES

Treating a Holocaust Survivor Without Addressing the Holocaust: A Case Report

Moshe Z. Abramowitz, MD
Pesach Lichtenberg, MD
Esther-Lee Marcus, MD
Baruch Shapira, MD

EDITOR'S INTRODUCTION TO THE CHAPTER: The case presented by Abramowitz et al. echoes some of the same points as the last case. Here a 63 year old woman's depression and suicide attempts were exacerbated by deteriorating inter-generational relationships. A combination of behavioral, cognitive, and supportive techniques served to strengthen her defenses and brought about a remission from her depression without addressing repressed issues of the Holocaust.

INTRODUCTION

Sometimes, psychodynamic formulations and a complete pharmacopoeia do not suffice to induce remission in a case of resistant

Moshe Z. Abramowitz is affiliated with the Psychiatry Department at the Hadassah University Hospital. Pesach Lichtenberg and Baruch Shapira are affiliated with the Psychiatry Department and Esther-Lee Marcus is affiliated with the Geriatric Department of the Sarah Herzog Memorial Hospital, P.O. Box 35300, Jerusalem 91351, Israel.

[Haworth co-indexing entry note]: "Treating a Holocaust Survivor Without Addressing the Holocaust: A Case Report." Abramowitz, Moshe Z. et al. Co-published simultaneously in the *Clinical Gerontologist* (The Haworth Press, Inc.) Vol. 14, No. 3, 1994, pp. 75-80; and: *Holocaust Survivors' Mental Health* (ed: T. L. Brink) The Haworth Press, Inc., 1994, pp. 75-80. Multiple copies of this article/chapter may be purchased from The Haworth Document Delivery Center [1-800-3-HAWORTH; 9:00 a.m. - 5:00 p.m. (EST)].

depression. Alternative approaches, taking into consideration the specific characteristics of the patient, must then be employed. We present a case where a consideration of the special needs of the patient precluded our addressing the Holocaust directly.

CASE REPORT

Ida, a 63 year-old married housekeeper and mother to three adult children, was hospitalized in the depression unit of the hospital with a diagnosis of major depression. Her illness had proven resistant to several courses of standard pharmacological treatment.

Two years before her admission, she had complained of restlessness and various somatic aches and pains. No organic disorder was found despite repeated physical diagnostic evaluations.

Eventually, a persistent, pervasive affect of sadness and depression set in, accompanied by an underlying sense of worthlessness and a yearning to die. Twice hospitalized for depression, she received combined anti-depressant and antipsychotic medication without any considerable change in mood. Six sessions of electroconvulsive therapy (ECT) were also administered, with a similar lack of results. After Ida attempted suicide by overdosing on her medications, she was transferred to our ward.

Ida was born to a middle-class Jewish family in a large city in pre-war Poland. Her father owned a garment store which provided an ample income for his wife and three daughters. Her mother was born and raised in Germany. Ida grew up in a modern, cultured atmosphere.

At the start of the Nazi occupation, Ida's father's store was confiscated, and the family's general situation deteriorated drastically. Subsequently, the Gestapo abducted Ida from her parents and sent her to a distant forced-labor camp. She was fifteen years old at the time.

Ultimately, her father and eldest sister perished at Auschwitz. Nothing is known about the fate of her mother and younger sister, but it is presumed that they suffered a similar doom.

After having spent most of the war in the camps, Ida found her way to a displaced-persons camp. She managed to study nursing there, and took responsibility for caring for the ill.

While still there, Ida met her future husband. He too had survived the Holocaust, having lost his entire family. The couple married and finally left for Israel in 1948, setting up home in a small town.

Ida and her husband had three children, two girls and a boy. During this period, she stopped working and devoted herself to her home and young children. Her daughters remember their mother as an energetic woman, always optimistic, and somewhat overindulgent of her children and grandchildren. No mention was ever made of life under Nazi occupation and in the camps.

There was no previous history of affective disorder, nor had psychological support ever been sought.

Upon admission, the mental status examination revealed severe agitation and a depressed affect, without any formal thought disorder. Hallucinations and delusions were absent. Ida had difficulty expressing her emotional state beyond a general statement of feeling bad and a plethora of somatic complaints. She spoke of suicide and death incessantly. Her general cognitive and intellectual performance was intact.

Careful questioning revealed that Ida's only son, during the year prior to the onset of Ida's depressive symptoms had adopted a strictly observant Jewish lifestyle, which had led him to distance himself from his parents. Ida insisted that her son could live however he chose, though her husband noted that Ida had always shown special concern for her son's wellbeing. Her son did not respond to our efforts to contact him.

A vigorous neuropsychiatric workup was conducted. Physical examination was unrevealing. Routine diagnostic blood tests, including a complete blood count, biochemical profile, and thyroid function tests, were normal. A C.T. scan of the brain was unremarkable.

Psychological testing emphasized the depressed affect. A recurrent theme on the projective tests was guilt pertaining to relations between family members. For example, one of the cards of the Thematic Apperception Test elicited a story of young children who were separated from their parents, and therefore responsible for the dismantling and destruction of their family.

The first three months of her hospitalization were marked by an intense effort to treat the "endogenous" component of the depression. A course of 16 ECT treatments was administered, and various combinations of anti-depressant medication and major tranquilizers (aimed at easing the agitation) were tried. As minimal improvement, if any, could be detected after these trials, a different strategy was adopted. Though psychotropic medication was maintained, the emphasis was placed on other aspects of her ailment.

Psychotherapy was conducted in an attempt to support the patient and legitimize her being well. Also, various *cognitive* elements were used to focus on generalizations of guilt thoughts and similar negative thoughts, bring them to the patient's attention and try to eliminate them and the accompanying affect.

Relaxation techniques were found to be very helpful to the patient and allowed her to continue the therapy at home with her husband. It provided a tool to be creatively used in concert with the husband and family, providing them for the first time with a measure of participation in and control of the situation.

Furthermore, once it was judged that the patient was no longer acutely suicidal, she was encouraged to set up her life again at home and to spend extended weekend vacations outside the hospital. For over two years she had been a "patient," and she viewed herself accordingly. Ida's husband became the focus of instruction and support. He helped nurture his wife's convalescence, assisted her, and calmed her when she was nervous.

In the few weeks following this change of tack, there was a considerable improvement in Ida's mood. She was more relaxed, revealed a dry, ironic sense of humor, and felt less guilty about her illness. She increasingly spent more time at home, and participated in the household chores. When she became overly anxious at home, as occasionally occurred, her husband would comfort her, and they would perform relaxation exercises in tandem. Within two months, she achieved a full remission and was discharged from the ward.

During a follow up period of three years, there was no relapse of depression. She remains on minimal doses of antidepressants.

DISCUSSION

Ida's depression, though developing over 40 years after the Holocaust, displayed many features of what has come to be known as the "survivor syndrome" (Niederland, 1968): survivor guilt, anxiety, depression, vegetative dysfunctions, and an inability to verbalize traumatic experiences.

Ida's clinical picture was also complicated by alexithymia, that is, an impairment in ability to express feelings and moods (Lesser, 1985). Though not uncommon in patients with a tendency to somatization and other psychiatric disorders (Taylor, 1984), alexithymia has also been attributed to the effects of severe trauma, as with Holocaust survivors (Krystal, 1982), where a masked depression may develop (Fisch, 1989).

One may speculate that the distancing of Ida's son may have played a role as a trigger of the depressive episode. Having and nurturing a family are important developmental processes with the potential for special regenerational effects for individuals who have lost their original family (Ornstein, 1981; Muller & Yahav, 1989). The perceived loss of a family member or of his love can therefore be particularly devastating for a survivor.

Ida's depression did not respond to conventional treatment. Having exhausted psychopharmacological attempts at inducing a remission, a parallel, multi-tiered strategy was employed.

Supportive psychotherapy with cognitive elements, relaxation technique, and family guidance and participation were instituted.

In light of Ida's alexithymic traits, we avoided psychodynamic psychotherapy, opting instead for a more direct, less intrusive approach. We attempted to *strengthen her defenses* by teaching her to cope with her anxiety. Respect was genuinely paid to Ida's long suffering and difficult past. Memories and issues relating to her experiences during her formative years, though very important, were not explored directly in the therapy. For example, we accepted Ida's attribution of guilt to her prolonged inactivity brought on by her illness; no attempt was made to relate this guilt to her survivor status.

Eventually, the long-awaited remission came about. Of course, we will never know if our efforts induced the remission or if the depression had simply run its course. Yet our sense is that while Ida's personality was not amenable to our directly addressing Ida's Holocaust experiences, we nevertheless gave her the possibility of overcoming some of her disability. The relaxation techniques allowed her to cope with her anxiety. Her husband's more active involvement restored some cohesion to her ruptured sense of family. Supportive psychotherapy helped her regain a measure of optimism. The fortunate result has been a durable and lasting period of mental health.

REFERENCES

Fisch, R. Z. (1989). Alexithymia, masked depression, and loss in a Holocaust survivor. *British Journal of Psychiatry, 154*, 708-710.

Krystal, H. (1982). Alexithymia and the effectiveness of psychoanalytic treatment. *International Journal of Psychoanalytic Psychotherapy, 9*, 353-378.

Lesser, I. M. (1985). Alexithymia. *New England Journal of Medicine, 312*, 690-692.

Muller, U. F., & Yahav, A. L. (1989). Object relations, Holocaust survival and family therapy. *British Journal of Medical Psychology, 62*, 13-21.

Niederland, W. (1968). The psychiatric evaluation of emotional disorders in survivors of Nazi persecution. In H. Krystal (Ed.), *Massive Psychic Trauma* (pp. 8-22). New York: International Universities Press.

Ornstein, A. (1981). The aging survivor of the Holocaust: the effects of the Holocaust on life-cycle experiences: the creation and recreation of families. *Journal of Geriatric Psychiatry, 14*, 135-154.

Taylor, G. J. (1984). Alexithymia: Concept, measurement, and implications for treatment. *American Journal of Psychiatry, 141*, 725-732.

Treatment of Elderly
Holocaust Survivors:
How Do Therapists Cope?

Sima Weiss, MSW
Dr. Natan Durst

EDITOR'S INTRODUCTION TO THE CHAPTER: Weiss and Durst address issues related to transference, countertransference and therapist burnout. Although their review of these issues in geriatrics is minimal, their application to work with this population are quite valuable. Their guidelines for a community-based therapy program are most useful for presenting a model which should improve outreach and prevention as well as reduce the burden placed on individual therapists.

During the aging stage, the 'third stage' of life, certain changes occur in one's body; in one's self-image in interhuman relationships, within the family cell, in intergenerational relationships; the need for medical attention and hospitalizations increases, as do organic problems; there is a cognitive decline, acknowledgement of loneliness and loss, and a need to deal with life's passages.

The loss of roles and of the ability to function also includes changes between the sexes, changes reflected in the methods of dealing with separation and loss, retirement, finding a meaning in

---

Mrs. Sima Weiss is Director, Ramat-Gan Branch, AMCHA. Dr. Natan Durst is Clinical Adviser, AMCHA/Ramat-Gan.

[Haworth co-indexing entry note]: "Treatment of Elderly Holocaust Survivors: How Do Therapists Cope?" Weiss, Sima and Natan Durst. Co-published simultaneously in the *Clinical Gerontologist* (The Haworth Press, Inc.) Vol. 14, No. 3, 1994, pp. 81-98; and: *Holocaust Survivors' Mental Health* (ed: T. L. Brink) The Haworth Press, Inc., 1994, pp. 81-98. Multiple copies of this article/chapter may be purchased from The Haworth Document Delivery Center [1-800-3-HAWORTH; 9:00 a.m. - 5:00 p.m. (EST)].

one's life. There is often a need to deal with a paranoid dynamic which is often seen as the primary problem of aging–depression, and, of course, dealing with death and all associated with it.

Prominent among the aging is reminiscing and reviewing one's life. This develops during the second half of one's life and can be observed in various mental processes, cognitive and temporal. *Reminiscence* is a part of reviewing one's life and occurs in the shadow of the awareness of finality and death. In reviewing one's life, which is characterized by remembrance of past experiences, especially those relating to unresolved conflicts an attempt is made at a renewed integration that, if successful, provides meaning to one's life and reduces the fear of death. Butler also states that this relates to a spontaneous human process, at times unconscious, that exists in every culture.

Given this background, it is important to state that the population of elderly Holocaust survivors dealt with here is characterized as all those who were under the Nazi regime and are now 63 years old and over. Those under that age fall within the category of child survivors.

Characteristics of the elderly Holocaust survivors today include: All experienced many losses, find themselves in extended bereavement–they have neither grave sites nor date of death, they did not mourn for the dead, nor did they sit 'Shiva' for them. There exists social isolation. In general, it can be stated that the overwhelming majority have functioned in an above-average manner over the years, and thus, as they get older, one can definitely discern survivors' symptoms, normal reactions to abnormal situations whose influence lasted for many years after the end of the war. There are many indications from a wide range of extreme situations, such as war, natural disasters or time in a concentration camp, that extreme pressure and stressful situations can bring about a wide range of physiological disturbances, illnesses and very evident psychological and social damage. However, if there is great similarity among the reactions to these situations, there are also major perceptual differences between a tragedy of human origins and those of a natural disaster. Furthermore, the fact that although not all victims of the Holocaust were Jews, but all Jews were its victims, obligates us to place Jewish Holocaust survivors in a separate and distinct category of victims of a tragedy of human origin.

One tragic characteristic of the Holocaust experience was the complete dehumanization of life while the threat of death constantly hovered above their heads, forcing the victims to witness the shattering of the basic principles by which they were raised, and to become used to a reality whose laws were absolutely meaningless. During the Holocaust people became mere numbers, without names. They lost all feelings of self-worth, self-confidence and trust in the individual. These psychological conditions which fall within the realm of a massive and cumulative trauma, forever changed their internal world and their way of life.

However, the makeup of the individual's prewar personality, the composition of his family, and the interfamilial relationships that existed before the Holocaust, as well as the victim's age at the start of the war, the details of the trauma and the individual's means of survival, all make up the survivor's post-traumatic personality and to a great extent determine his reactions. It must also be remembered that in order to maintain their sanity in an insane world, the Holocaust victims had to build within themselves a thick defensive wall when more than once their natural defenses proved insufficient to protect themselves from ongoing damage.

Furthermore, part of the trauma of the Holocaust was the loss of relatives and the uprooting of the victim from his home and community. This situation continued even after the war, when most of the survivors still had nowhere to go, no home to return to, and thus many remained in the displaced person camps in Germany, before being sent to their new home. This terrible situation was called by Matusek, 'double uprooting'–that is, from family and from community, without home and without possessions–with the necessity to start everything from scratch in a new country, with a new culture and new language. And even there, whether it was their country of birth that had so totally changed, a new country, or even Israel, survivors were greeted with complete and total misunderstanding.

Proof of this can be seen in the statement of an AMCHA* client, Chaim, 66 years old, Hungarian born, a survivor of Auschwitz:

---

*The National Israeli Center for Psychosocial Support of Survivors of the Holocaust and the Second Generation

> After wandering around Germany for two years, I arrived in Israel with Youth Aliyah and was sent to a kibbutz. They put me in a group with children from Yugoslavia since they were also from Eastern Europe, but they had not been in the camps, they did not speak German, and thus we had no common language. In class they called me 'soap.' At first I did not understand what the word meant. It was only after I learned the meaning of the word that I hit one of the children until he realized that he could not insult my parents that way.

This testimony indicates how poor the treatment of or consideration towards the individual's personal trauma was, and to what extent society was involved in the "Conspiracy of Silence."

The awareness of the psychosocial impact of the Holocaust on its survivors was gradually concretized as the years passed. For a long period, professionals did not recognize the essence of the phenomena related to this trauma. This non-awareness also stemmed from the shock that overcame the professionals themselves when they heard these stories, so horrifying and unprecedented. In either case the survivors did not receive proper treatment immediately after their liberation, which led to the early fixation of the survivors' psychological isolation, and, later, even to passing on the symptomology to their descendants, the second generation.

In order to clarify this fixation, we can see the testimony of Suzy, 68, a Polish-born client, also a survivor of Auschwitz:

> As a young girl, I married another survivor immediately after the war. He was ill for many years and died when our son was 14. . . . I knew what to do. After that my mother, who had miraculously survived the war, passed away. Then, again, I knew what to do. I remarried, to a nice man. Everything seemed fine. The children were healthy and growing. What more could I ask for? But things are not fine with me. I always knew how to survive, *but I had never learned how to live.*

In situations such as this, one minor incident is sufficient to raise the pressure and produce a mental and physical imbalance in the survivor. He might then be referred to a physician who might not always know how to reach the root of the survivor's anxieties and depression, which in fact lies in his traumatic past that had never previously been dealt with.

When survivors were released from the camps, a period of repression and denial began, with the primary need being to forget the past, and reorganize anew by developing and expanding activities in all areas of their lives, just as long as they no longer had to deal with their pasts. Sublimating the traumas of the past turned this past into an unnatural aspect of the survivors psyche, but one which continued to exist within many of these survivors in their dreams. Often, however, this feature also ceased, but many of them discovered that their will power was not sufficient to withstand the repressed memories, the intolerable thoughts that returned to haunt them. As early as 1946, a Dutch psychiatrist named Tess, wrote of the difficulty survivors had in everything relating to expressing anger or feelings that arose as a result of their wartime experiences. Even then he claimed that this phenomenon would slow the process of uncovering the client's inner self and would make his treatment more difficult, assuming that the survivor would in fact seek such treatment. Tess was the first to reach these conclusions and he was convinced that changes in the physical and economic makeup influenced the survivor's vitality as he grew older. Furthermore, even their approaching death could lead to the exacerbation of the influence of these repressed feelings, and lead the survivor to seek help and treatment.

Here, for example, are the words of Ilana, aged 70, married and the mother of three, born in Czechoslovakia:

> The first time I went for treatment I was 35, a short time after the birth of my daughter (born after two sons). I couldn't stop crying, and all that time all I wanted was my mother who had died in the Holocaust.
>
> They told me, "Look, you know why you're crying so much. It's healthy, it's natural and it will pass." They sent me home. I got over it; did I have a choice?
>
> The second time was in 1958. I was then 48 years old and they told me: "Madame, there is a convergence here of two things–menopause and tension relating to the Yom Kippur War. You're strong, and, anyway, the Holocaust ended years ago, and you must forget it." They gave me some pills and I

got over it. . . . How many times does a person have to yell for help before he is heard? Now I have stopped working, but I am no longer sure if anyone can help me.

She reached AMCHA highly motivated but suspicious because of the many previous disappointments. Treatment within AMCHA was conducted based on the following specialized models:

1. Treatment based on the client's needs.
2. Opening a 'Pandora's Box' holding repressed experiences, memories and tears. Working through the mourning–opening the box firmly, but carefully.
3. Setting one's inner chaos in order.
4. Integration.
5. Individuation.
6. Increasing awareness of the "self" as part and parcel of the family and feeling a part of society.

The convergence of lack of awareness, ignorance and fear on the part of the psychiatric community, together with the survivor's strong desire to cut himself off from the past, led, therefore, to a great deal of excess suffering.

However, even today, as young members of the second generation come in for treatment, there is simultaneously a new generation of therapists who do not know how to treat them. This new generation must be warned against the widespread generalization that all Holocaust survivors are ill, pitiful or unbalanced. It is sufficient that we remember Epstein's theory on this matter, that most Holocaust survivors functioned as normal and healthy individuals, raised families and even survived several wars in Israel, some even losing children in these wars. Therefore, even Epstein herself criticizes the picture drawn in the professional literature, films, etc., of the survivor as a "nebech" or a lost cause. The greatest injustice is to overlook the tremendous inner strength that many survivors uncovered within themselves when they started again from nothing, exhibiting vigor and vitality in creativity and activity in all areas of their lives.

THE CLIENT IN TREATMENT

In order for the therapeutic process to proceed successfully, some important characteristics are demanded of the client. He must be able to deal with recent as well as distant events, to deal with dependence and independence, and to uncover his inner self. The specialized situations encountered in treatment awaken in many survivors a desire to be seen as individuals by the therapist. Holocaust survivors, on whom a tag of 'irregular' was attached long ago, are liable to demand excess attention by the therapist.

Two conflicting desires show themselves in the reactions to treatment—a desire to forget vs. a desire to remember. These conflicts create an inner tension, to the client's unclear position and to disagreements during the course of treatment. It must be remembered in any cage that this sort of ambivalence towards the treatment process exists within the client as well as the therapist.

Survivors, living in emotional isolation, find it difficult to place their trust in individuals and feel threatened by an intimate relationship as a result of their Holocaust experiences. Therefore, it is probable that they will initially try to reject the therapist's offer of help, and may even express aggression towards the therapist, as a defensive tactic. The more intensively this aggression is displayed on the part of the client, the greater his cry for help.

Survivors often show signs of early aging, which often arouses additional fears as the defense system weakens and as the ability to perform compulsively strenuous work lessens. Feelings of inferiority then develop that awaken past traumas, which are seen as a threat, as something they are unable to deal with, since the survivor had learned long ago that a display of weakness meant capitulating to the enemy.

Frequently, the client comes for treatment with exaggerated expectations from the therapist, who has a similar background: The therapist will understand him in any case and thus there is no need to speak excessively. At the same time, there exists in the treatment room fears of abandonment, repression and hurt and, even worse, a fear of being misunderstood by the therapist. Thus, many difficult hours lie ahead for the client as well as the therapist once it becomes clear that there is no alternative but to come face to face with the realities of the past. These hours are difficult primarily because of the fear of opening the Pandora's Box, because of the look backward that might turn those doing so–if one may use the Biblical metaphor–to pillars of salt. Thus, the beginning of treatment with survivors is very slow and demands establishing a base of mutual trust because of the reluctance to open those deep wounds filled with pain, great hurt and humiliation.

In his book *Night,* Elie Weisel writes of the long road he and his father traveled until reaching Buchenwald. Throughout the trip, he cared for his sick father and thought: "Would that I could free myself from this dead weight so that I could use all my strength to save myself and look after myself." And immediately afterwards: "I felt ashamed of myself, an eternal shame." Towards the end of the book he adds: "After I recovered, I looked in the mirror, and saw a corpse facing me. The look in its eyes–the look with which it looked at me then–will never leave me." These words underline the feeling of humiliation that is created in situations when a man feels that his existence is threatened by another man who, to him, seems all-powerful. Furthermore, a man feels ashamed when he must do things for which he will feel shame later on. *A feeling of humiliation* similar to this is aroused, in addition to feelings of *anger and helplessness,* in the heart of the client, towards the person before whom he now feels ashamed: the therapist.

Thus, even this humiliation is liable to become a factor delaying treatment, and even preventing it from reaching a conclusion. A good example is that of Hannah, born in 1937 who first came for treatment in 1974 as a result of difficulties in her 11-year-old son's schooling. In the screening interview she mentioned that she had been imprisoned in a labor camp during the war with her entire family, and that all were eventually released from there, healthy and whole. She was unwilling to elaborate on details of that period since, in fact, according to her, she did not undergo any trauma at all. I, on my part, agreed to her request and did not dig further.

She returned twice more, each time for short-term treatment, resulting from family crises. In late 1984, she telephoned, hysterical, from a hospital, where she had been admitted for treatment of back problems which included receiving spinal injections. She broke down then, unable to stop crying. She disclosed that during the war she and her twin brother had been imprisoned in Auschwitz where they underwent experimentation by Dr. Mengele, including various injections, among others, in her back. She was the sole surviving family member. After the war she was adopted by distant relatives.

When classmates had persisted in badgering her about the number tattooed on her arm, her adoptive father decided to have it removed, saying that "she has nothing to be proud of." These facts made it easier for her to hide her past life from her children and friends. Today, after the repressed trauma was brought to the surface once again, she has begun to deal with the various feelings buried within her, including a feeling of deep humiliation.

THE TREATMENT ROOM

People who have experienced massive and cumulative traumas are likely to behave with *aggression, dependence and excessive attachment.* In addition, treatment work with survivors is difficult and complicated, especially considering their overwhelming need for love. They exhibit suspicion, mistrust and internalized projections onto the individual, expressed, among other ways, in sentences such as: "When I look backwards I don't understand–am I talking of a nightmare or of my actual experiences? And if *I* don't understand, or can't express it in words, how can *you* understand or help me?" Comments such as these reflect the psychological baggage loaded onto the therapist in this specific circumstance, as he hesitates to treat survivors because of their negative prognosis and severe disturbance, in addition to a feeling of his own helplessness as well as that towards the advancing age of the client group.

The words of de Wind should he recalled here, whereby the psychological investment of the therapist in the survivor client is similar to treatment of borderline patients, that is, five treatment hours per one for a regular client, since *it is so difficult to listen to the stories of horrors and atrocities such as those experienced by the survivors, without the therapist himself experiencing trauma.*

Most of those researching Holocaust experiences and their delayed psychological effects come from the analytical school. Chodoff, included in this group, summarized the professional literature relating to the effectiveness of psychoanalytic therapy on Holocaust survivors, and reached a discouraging conclusion: Since the disturbances of the survivor are so extreme, treating him is that much more difficult and limited. Any change or correction is liable to occur only as a result of intensive, long-term treatment, in his words, and even this is highly doubtful, since successful treatment of survivors occurs primarily when treating those who experienced their traumas as adults.

This review draws a very pessimistic picture which, it seems, probably influenced a great many therapists who hesitate or even refuse to treat Holocaust survivors. However, Chodoff's reliable yet pessimistic viewpoint is put into question when faced with the fact that most of the material published regarding the Holocaust syndrome is based primarily on clinical treatment and on research conducted in psychiatric hospitals which, naturally, deal with a very specific population. It is important to remember that one cannot really relate to the survivor population as a homogeneous group. Each survivor is different in the history of his experiences, his suffering and his loss, and in the effect of the Holocaust on him, as well as his ability to deal with it.

In light of the fact that the survivor's basic trust relating to interpersonal relations is systematically subverted, the therapist is faced with a unique challenge regarding the client: The need to build a framework of trust with the client in this specific instance is contraindicated in terms of a formal approach or a restrained, distanced position.

Many times, it turns out that the situation dealt with is that of long-term treatment, including providing support. The time factor plays an important part in the development of this process, since it allows the development of a cathartic process in a repeated and cumulated manner. In an atmosphere of acceptance and empathy, understanding and tolerance, the client can release some of his pent-up emotions (such as aggression, for example), as well as the repressed bereavement within him. On the other hand, the therapist must thus become personally involved in the treatment process and thus minimize the distance usually placed between himself and the client. Instead of placing himself opposite the client, he must project a feeling of solidarity in the client's battle with his ongoing pain, with his search for new roads by which he will hopefully learn to live with his wounds and at the same time still find meaning in his life.

These themes can he concretized by the following case: After two years of treatment and an ongoing struggle between us, the client, a 68-year-old female survivor presented me with a painting she had done, representing a baby with the name of "Hope." The baby in the picture is small, delicate and fragile. . . .

People who have lied for so many years, both to themselves and others, need a great deal of patience in order to finally build a life of truth based on honesty, openness and trust. An example: Gila, born in Poland in 1937, lived in hiding for three years with a Polish farmer. During the summer she stayed in a deep pit in the yard, and during winter in the attic. Following the war, she moved to Israel with her aunt, did well in High School and the army, got an MA, married and had two children. Despite all this, she began to suffer from depression and came to AMCHA suffering from amnesia regarding the Holocaust period. At one of the sessions when she talked about her isolation, I tried, using psychodrama, to help her "emerge from the pit." I extended my hand to her and asked her to believe in me and give me her hand. She didn't dare. I persisted; I begged. She sat back on her heels, her arms around her legs. It took some time before she dared move to the middle of the "pit," and there she stayed. I cried. . . . over her helplessness, and mine. Did I fail . . . ? Was I wrong . . . ?

Professional literature places special emphasis on countertransference among Holocaust survivors. It is natural that the client himself will experience strong feelings and reactions. Danieli prefers to call these reactions 'transference,' since they stem from the fact that the therapist reacts in an extreme manner to the client's description of his wartime experiences. However from research she conducted among survivors, she found that these reactions were independent from the sessions with the client, and were actually pre-existent.

Among the "reactions" or countertransference, we mention the following:

1. Feelings of guilt: They suffered, and as a result the therapist is more careful in his attitude toward the client.

2. Anxiety and disgust as a result of the stories of atrocities, and as a result, a more objective stance, searching traumas in their youth or in the present.
3. Sadness and pity in face of the deep bereavement: Feelings that lead to overidentification on the one hand or distancing on the other.
4. Helplessness: A possible reaction to the client's need for control by the therapist.
5. Anger (complaints, accusations): Postponement or cessation of treatment, etc.

It should be stated that these reactions are within the realm of honest human emotions of fear and aversion to the atrocities that have been running after the client even up to the present.

Insufficient attention has been placed over the years on the topic of psychological treatment of Holocaust survivors, and an insufficient amount of attention and support has been given to it, both in formal training and in specialized supervision. This was true until five years ago, when AMCHA was established by a group of Holocaust survivors who believed that the time had come for Israeli society to deal in a specialized and differential way with the Holocaust survivor population and their psychosocial needs. Especially today, when most survivors have reached their golden years, the age when their pasts play such crucial roles in their lives, the AMCHA center was founded.

Two basic goals stand at the source of AMCHA establishment:

1. To increase awareness among professionals; therapists; people having contact with the Holocaust survivor population in hospitals, health funds, old age homes, clinics and social service departments. To bring to these people's attention the fact that Holocaust survivors are aging. The essence of this aging process is a trigger that arouses repressed memories and experiences that create agitation in the client's inner world, as mentioned above. Defense mechanisms that were partially functional over the years become less so and we now find the aging Holocaust survivor in situations of tremendous pressure, depression, crisis and even lack of will to live.
2. Breaking the conspiracy of silence that has characterized the state and people of Israel. AMCHA's establishment is clear

proof that this conspiracy of silence can and must be broken and in its place comes the need and desire of both sides to listen and be heard. And this is the individual treatment that survivors and their children receive.

This is the place to emphasize that each survivor is a separate individual, different from his neighbor, carrying within himself his own personal baggage, specific to him. For purposes of discussion it is possible to categorize types of 'baggage' that survivors carry from the period of the Holocaust, including painful loads such as face-to-face meetings with death, massive loss, extermination of entire families, fear, degradation of one's self-esteem, attempts to estrange them from their humanity, efforts to separate them from their basic human needs, as well as the need for respect, love, intimate relationships, mutual trust.

Some survivors have tried over the years to tell their stories and to express what they were going through. They wrote books, scripted plays, directed productions, painted, photographed, composed, all these to stem the overflowing feelings they were trying to express; but not everyone could express their feelings in these ways. There was still something missing in personal relationships with a sensitive partner who was prepared to listen to the stories and share with the teller all the varied, sensitive and intimate details. This is the intimate and legitimate "together" to which the survivor strives through the years.

The lack of this feeling is most obvious during times of pressure and crisis, with both subject to internal distress, such as loss of a spouse and retirement that normally occur with aging. The human contact between the elderly survivor and the therapist is a challenge in itself. We must remember that Nazism deeply affected the survivor's desire and ability to trust another human being. The world was seen as hostile and cruel and thus the survivor's difficulty to establish intimate relationships with and trust others even after the war ended is quite understandable.

Attempts at AMCHA to connect with these aging survivors are an opportunity for the survivor to attempt to develop a close relationship that includes within it a calming influence, identification and understanding. This closeness represents the basis for renewing one's trust in one's fellow man, while at the same time reducing the feeling of loneliness and providing hope for a better life, during one's later years.

Two specialized programs have been developed at AMCHA to help elderly Holocaust survivors:

1. *Documentation of personal testimonies* is one program offered to clients of AMCHA. The opportunity for the elderly survivor to discuss his wartime experiences is often accompanied by difficulties of great pain and opening of long-closed wounds. We see in the recording of the survivor's personal history a useful means to organize the many varied and heavy memories that have been flooding through the survivor's mind and to make them more bearable during his retirement years and as he is forced to deal with his aging and separation from his children.

We also receive requests from children of survivors to interview their parents, something that has become a necessity for them, but they nonetheless find it difficult to do on their own because of a fear of the emotional impact this would have in their relationship with their parents.

For many survivors, the connection between various traumatic periods from their youth remains hazy, and they are often cut off from the specific effects of these events on their own lives. Providing an organized testimony, moderated by a professional therapist returns their personal identity to them when the connection between their past experiences before, during and after the war, and their present-day experiences and reactions is clarified.

When we sit with survivors and moderate a documentation session of their testimony, we create a unique and intimate experience of complete and total attention, empathy and support as they have not received perhaps since the Holocaust years themselves. As a result, they uncover and discuss experiences they have lived, many of the most traumatic and difficult to describe, most have probably not been shared with another person since the day they were experienced.

It is natural that those of us who are witness to these testimonies project a silent preparedness to accompany the interviewee without any treatment limitations or interventions, and paying complete attention to the story being told. We are aware of the strong impact that these testimonies represent for us. Each interviewer must be aware of his/her own individual limitations regarding the quantity of these atrocities that he has the strength to hear.

This documentation raises events and memories that had been hidden in the survivor's mind through all these years. Most of them managed to find the inner strength to establish families and new lives, and deserve and need our appreciation for this strength as well as our restraint when they include us in revealing the most difficult details of their past. Most survivors avoid pathos as they tell their stories; this testimony differs from a newspaper interview or simple verification of historical facts, and even from a therapy session. The broader goal of taping one's personal testimony is that at the end, the survivor is left with the cassettes in hand that hold his individual testimony, and of which he can make whatever use he desires.

Thus, talking about the Holocaust represents a tremendous need during aging, out of an inner need to tell the story for future generations, something which a large number of survivors have been unable to do until today.

2. *The Social/Treatment Club* for older survivors is a unique response that developed in AMCHA during the course of recognizing the emotional/social needs of the older Holocaust survivor. An awareness of this population and review of existing professional literature dealing with research into trauma raised the strong need among many of them to participate in social meetings wherein the Holocaust theme would not necessarily be a central one, but that nonetheless would meet at AMCHA and would be composed of fellow survivors.

The rationale is the survivors' need to participate in an enabling and supportive atmosphere where it is legitimate to be a survivor with a foreign accent and a number tattooed on one's forearm. The enjoyment of this experience is reflected in a vitality and connection to life and one's strengths.

Out of this rationale we have inferred several specific goals:

1. Establishment of a club that will represent both an informal and a formal meeting place, a home for survivors with a social bent, without any therapeutic obligations and all that infers.
2. To provide an answer to the feelings of loneliness and isolation that are common phenomena among the elderly in general and seen more widely among Holocaust survivors in particular as one characteristic of the post-traumatic personality.
3. To provide an answer to the strong, unanswered need to relate to other people. It must he remembered that one of the characteristics of the Holocaust was the individual's total separation from his roots, family and home, the massive loss of life's meaning and becoming the epitome of the wandering and persecuted Jew. Thus, the club becomes for them a place to finally belong.
4. To act as a bridge and make clients in theory to clients in practice, a connecting link with a non-demanding social orientation and perhaps at the same time to bring them closer to actual treatment.
5. To be used as a basis for examining the possibility of establishing self-help groups stemming from the club's membership.
6. The fact that the club is located in the AMCHA center is itself a treatment element that provides backing and legitimization for those who visit the club and who know that they can come in short sleeves to expose their number without hiding or being ashamed of their pasts.
7. The regularity and permanence of this framework–meetings are held regularly twice a week in the club's regular room at the AMCHA center–is a source of stability for people who had lost a sense of control over their lives. The feeling of security that this framework will continue on a regular basis, even, for example, during the period of the Gulf War, and during holiday periods that are celebrated together in place of one's family that is no more. The possibility to regularly meet with fellow survivors, hear lectures, go on trips and even talk together about painful things when one feels like it, within the context of the club that is supervised by professionals ever-

ready to help, represents a unique opportunity for survivors who see this as their home. As a result, feelings of self-respect take the place of the sense of strangeness and shame they had previously felt as members of the Israel society.

SUMMARY

Treatment of survivors teaches us to become more modest in our goals, since more than once the help we could provide ends with participating in the client's feelings of helplessness, as well as experiencing a mutual learning experience, wherein feelings of shame and guilt are an inseparable part of our reality.

In addition, we must turn our attention to members of the second generation who were educated by survivors but who did not succeed in acquiring for themselves feelings of self-confidence. Like their parents, they too had to deal with death and meaninglessness in their lives, as well as with problems of communication, loneliness, emptiness and hopelessness. They can benefit from our therapeutic support as long as we do not repeat our past mistakes regarding the 'conspiracy of silence' of the previous generation of therapists. Brill has already stated that ". . . responsibilities stemming from our profession and our loyalty to all, obligate us to devote ourselves unreservedly to our work." Further: "Since the future is unknown it arouses dread. But if we transform the future from something fateful that may happen to something that we can create, then we transform the future into one of hope. Despite the awareness of our mortality–the future depends on us."

REFERENCES

1. Axelrod, Snipper and Rau: "Hospitalized offspring of Holocaust survivors; problems and dynamics," *Bull. Menninger Clinic.* 1980 (I), 1-14.

2. Chodoff, P: "Psychiatric aspects of the Nazi-persecution," *Amer. Handbook of Psychiatry,* 1975 (6), 991-1000.

3. Danieli, Y: "Countertransference in the treatment and study of Nazi Holocaust survivors and their children," *Victimology.* 1961 (3), 345-368.

4. Epstein, H: *Children of the Holocaust.* NY: Putnam, 1979.

5. Lifton, R: "On death and Holocaust: Some thoughts on survivors," in *Group Analysis; the Survivor Syndrome Workshop.* London: 1980, 13-23.

6. Matussek, P: *Die Konzentrationslager und Ihre Folgen.* Berlin: Springer, 1971.

7. Wiesel, E: *Night.* NY: Avon, 1969.

8. Wind, E. de: "Psychoanalytische behandeling van ernstig getraumatiseerden door verolging en verzet," *Tijdd. Psychotherapie.* 1982 (3), 143-155.

9. Tas, J: Psychische stoornissen in oncentratiekampen en bij teruggekeerden," *Maankbl. Geest. Volksqezondheid,* 1946, 143-150.

10. Brill, B (Bedereh le'Psychoterapia Humanistit) (Hebrew). *The Way to Humanistic Psychotherapy.* A. Levin-Epstein-Modan, 1974.

11. Davidson, S (Tipul Benitzolei HaShoa, Betoh T'humei Pe'ilut Psihoterapeutit) (Hebrew). *The Treatment of Holocaust Survivors in Psychotherapeutic Settings,* ed. S. Davidson. Haifa. 1973.

Holocaust Survivors
in a Jewish Nursing Home:
Building Trust
and Enhancing Personal Control

Kathryn Betts Adams, MSW
Ellen Steinberg Mann, MSW
Rebecca Weintraub Prigal, MSW
Adele Fein, MSW
Trisha L. Souders, MSW
Barbara Sookman Gerber, MSW

EDITOR'S INTRODUCTION TO THE CHAPTER: Adams et al. use five case studies to demonstrate how group and milieu strategies can be employed in long term care. These patients had many problems commonly found in this population: paranoia and anxiety around changes. The recommended emphases on building trust and enhancing personal control are excellent strategies in any long term care facility.

INTRODUCTION

Geriatric clinicians consider individuals' particular life crises in assessing their adaptation to aging with its inherent changes and

Kathryn Betts Adams, Ellen Steinberg Mann, Rebecca Weintraub Prigal, Adele Fein, and Trisha L. Souders are social workers. Barbara Sookman Gerber is Assistant Director of Social Services at The Hebrew Home of Greater Washington, 6121 Montrose Road, Rockville, MD 20852.

[Haworth co-indexing entry note]: "Holocaust Survivors in a Jewish Nursing Home: Building Trust and Enhancing Personal Control." Adams, Kathryn Betts et al. Co-published simultaneously in the *Clinical Gerontologist* (The Haworth Press, Inc.) Vol. 14, No. 3, 1994, pp. 99-117; and: *Holocaust Survivors' Mental Health* (ed: T. L. Brink) The Haworth Press, Inc., 1994, pp. 99-117. Multiple copies of this article/chapter may be purchased from The Haworth Document Delivery Center [1-800-3-HA-WORTH; 9:00 a.m. - 5:00 p.m. (EST)].

losses. At the Hebrew Home of Greater Washington, a 550 bed, non-profit long term care facility in Rockville, Maryland, we have come to recognize the monumental impact of the Holocaust, superimposed upon each individual's life history. As social workers, we work with a Jewish population whose attitudes, world view and sense of security were all deeply affected by the Holocaust. In this paper, however, we focus on a few of our residents whose lives were directly touched by this tragic chapter in history, having lived in Europe just prior to or during World War II. Taking our definition from Trachtenberg and Davis, we consider Holocaust survivors, ". . . those individuals who lived through the concentration camps, work camps, ghettos or in hiding; or those who were driven into exile, as was the case with Eastern European Jews who sought refuge in Russia and German Jews who fled prior to the imposition of Hitler's final solution" (1978, p. 294). The case studies presented in this paper illustrate the special-psychosocial issues of Holocaust survivors in nursing homes and interventions directed to meet some of their specific emotional needs.

A number of authors have documented the effects of the Holocaust experience on aging survivors (Carmelly, 1975; Conrad, 1969; Harel & Kahana, 1988; Hertz, 1990; Kuch & Cox, 1992; Robinson, Rapaport, Durst, Rapaport, Rosca, Metzer & Zilberman, 1990; Rosenbloom, 1983; Steinitz, 1984; Trachtenberg & Davis, 1978). Aging survivors have been found to suffer from PostTraumatic Stress Disorder (Kuch & Cox, 1992) and to have high incidences of depression and anhedonia, acute anxiety, particularly around change, psychosomatic disturbances, sleep disturbances, and chronic guilt feelings (Conrad, 1969; Carmelly, 1975; Robinson et al., 1990). Mistrust is a common problem and may be severe enough to be considered a paranoid reaction (Rosenbloom, 1983; Steinitz, 1984; Trachtenberg & Davis, 1978). Holocaust survivors frequently experience loneliness and isolation, often manifested by difficulty in communicating the traumatic events to others including close family members (Conrad, 1969; Steinitz, 1984).

Entry into a nursing home is likely to be a difficult experience for anyone (Meunier & Schulz, 1991) but especially so for the Holocaust survivor who brings a unique bereavement history. Leaving long-time homes, beloved possessions, and loved ones behind is part of the "normal" nursing home admission experience. When entering the nursing home, most residents are forced to confront their mortality, on some level, acknowledging that this is their last stop, their last residence before death. For the survivor, this is not the first experience with loss of home and family to go to a strange, frightening place which may represent imminent danger or death. The memories of horror from their Holocaust experience remain with the survivor and old fearful feelings may be reawakened as they enter the nursing home. "Illness, hospitalization, or institutionalization may reawaken dormant Holocaust-related feelings about helplessness, regimentation and powerlessness" (Rosenbloom, 1983, p. 212). Nursing home placement is often seen as a last resort for aging survivors, making the final decision an agonizing one for the elder and the involved family members. According to Steinitz, for those children of frail elderly survivors requiring long term care, there is "avoidance of situations where (the survivor-parent is) helpless, out of control . . . (and an) avoidance of nursing homes because of similarity to the camps (i.e., a totally controlled institution) . . . [h]ome care (is) seen as safer, less threatening than institutionalization" (1984, p. 336). The Holocaust survivor, therefore, may have more difficulty at the time of admission because institutionalization represents a loss, a change in status, a separation, and possibly abandonment all of which recall earlier trauma and produce a sense of loss of personal control (Rosenbloom, 1983; Conrad, 1969; Steinitz, 1984).

Perceived personal control is one predictor of psychological well-being in nursing home residents (Bowsher & Gerlach, 1990). The clinical literature reports that several types of nursing home residents have been found to respond positively to interventions designed to offer choices and some measure of control over their environment (Blumenfeld, 1982; Burr, 1986; Raber, Lamboo & Mitchell-Pederson, 1986; Zarit, Zarit, & Rosenberg-Thompson, 1990). For example, Raber et al. found remarkable improvement in a difficult and uncooperative patient after staff spent one day providing her with intensive attention focused on allowing her to be entirely in control of her day's activities (1986). Zarit et al. described staff interactions with Alzheimer's patients which attempted to provide control to a confused population and minimized disruptive behaviors (1990). Blumenfeld (1982) offered choice of appointment times and had staff allow an angry, non-compliant female patient to decide when to be up and what snacks to eat. The patient reportedly came to cooperate with necessary medical procedures.

As survivors adjust to nursing home placement they, like all residents, must deal with the authority figures, regimented schedules, close living quarters, central shower areas, and other institutional realities that have special meaning for them. In addition, their life experience has included struggle against external threats to their well-being and internal despair. The coping strategies utilized by these residents in advanced age undoubtedly represent some of the mechanisms that emerged during the war years. These strategies may or may not be constructively adaptive in the nursing home setting.

As a member of an interdisciplinary team, the social worker assesses the residents' needs, struggles, and coping abilities and intervenes as is clinically indicated to enable the best adjustment possible. The case studies here present five different residents with certain commonalities to their backgrounds and the problems they have experienced in the nursing home. Some of the themes are familiar from the Holocaust survivor literature, particularly mistrust, sense of persecution, isolation, anxiety, and stubborn self-neglect. Two of the residents described have died and the way they chose to die was intrinsically linked to their psychological condition and very probably to the emotional damage suffered during the Holocaust. The other three residents remain at the Hebrew Home as of this writing, experiencing the usual fluctuations in adjustment. Staff interventions with these particularly challenging residents emphasize building trust and offering personal control in the nursing home.

THE CASES

Dora: "Like I'm in a jungle . . . "

Dora,* now in her 80s, was born in Russia and lived there through World War II. Suspicious of the German's plans, she and another family member escaped from their home to a safe area during the war. She recalls that those Jews who believed the Ger-

---

*Names and some identifying details have been changed.

mans were still good were killed. For Dora, distrust has meant survival. This suspiciousness and sense that people are not worthy of her trust has lingered into Dora's later adult life. Such paranoid reactions are characteristic of Holocaust survivors described in the mental health literature (Steinitz, 1984; Trachtenberg and Davis, 1978). More than thirty of Dora's family members were not wary of the Germans and were killed in the war, including her husband who died in the army.

Dora never had any children but has a host of nieces and nephews who are most attentive to her. Though she worked in Russia, she never worked in the U.S. She was a homemaker who spent leisure time reading, watching TV and going to shows.

The decision to come to the Hebrew Home was met with tremendous ambivalence by this mentally intact woman with diagnoses of Parkinson's disease, osteoporosis, degenerative joint disease and major depression, with history of suicidal ideation. A hip fracture was the precipitating event that "allowed" Dora to accept nursing home placement. Prior to that crisis, Dora demonstrated an obsessive need to make the "best decision" possible, symptomatic of the passive guilt of many survivors (Carmelly, 1975). Carmelly also points out that the fear and anxiety surrounding changes can be quite intense for the survivor. Dora's ambivalence and anxiety have only been matched by her neediness and underlying sadness as she struggles to adapt to an institutional setting.

When invited to a group meeting or activity, Dora rarely accepts. Her low self-esteem, sense of worthlessness and social inadequacy (Carmelly, 1975; Steinitz, 1984) seem to keep her apart from others despite her intelligence and verbal ability (she has an accent but is quite articulate). When Dora does attend a group, she prefers to sit as close to the door as possible and seems apart from the group as if she will not allow herself to become fully involved or to be too far from access to an exit. Social work and activity staff are attuned to her special needs in group settings, including her choice of seating and how long she will stay at a group. Dora is most responsive to a Russian speaking volunteer who visits regularly. She also appreciates the visits of another resident to her room where they can talk in the setting most familiar to Dora.

In individual supportive sessions, Dora's social worker allowed

Dora the choice of when to meet and the opportunity to rehash old complaints and issues before addressing more current concerns. This control seemed to provide some comfort and release if only until the next of their frequent sessions. In his book describing what enables people to come out of traumatic experiences, such as living in captivity, with some degree of mental health, Julius Segal writes, "In choosing to interact with others rather than withdrawing into ourselves, we are demonstrating a willingness to do something about our suffering–to control our fate. And it is this sense of personal control that turns out to be one of the most important characteristics of those who, in the end, prevail over life's adversities" (Segal, 1986, p. 29). Some connection with a trusted other to whom she could communicate without fear of judgment was critical to Dora's ability to cope with the burdens of her past and the stress of institutional living.

When speaking of her experience in Europe and of her lost relatives, Dora seems more genuine than in other interactions. It is as if she must otherwise operate in her defended, depressed manner, demanding of staff and dissatisfied with herself and others, in order to maintain some kind of familiar survival mode. Only with slow, consistent efforts at trust building has Dora come to allow select staff to see her smile and has she been able to accept their kindnesses. Ongoing complaints and undoing of any solutions presented by staff have contributed to rising frustration and polarization between Dora and many other staff. Staff who have "succeeded" with Dora have done so by accepting and understanding that her negativity and suspiciousness are a response to the trauma of her past. These caring staff are also able to allow Dora control whenever possible and to avoid internalizing her endless criticisms. Staff education meetings emphasizing sensitivity to Dora's past have been most helpful in this regard.

Specific examples of Dora's depressive and "paranoid" reactions include her response to other residents and to staff's treatment of her as compared to other residents. She persistently complains that she gets the least attention of any resident on the unit. She particularly focuses on attentive care to her roommate as compared to her own neglect by staff. The sense of persecution and worthlessness is quite pervasive and difficult to alter. The most effective treatment has been the frequent supportive attention paid to her by staff in tune with Dora's neediness. These staff are those that Dora refers to as "saints" or "gems." When those staff have a day off, Dora has a bad day, a day when she will state that she feels "like I am in a jungle," or question, "Am I in a concentration camp or a Jewish organization?" Bridging this gap is an ongoing process of allowing Dora maximum control and offering consistent, attentive demonstrations of concern.

Lottie: "Treated like a prisoner."

Lottie, born in 1906 in Germany, was in her mid-twenties, already engaged to be married and living in Vienna, when a Jewish organization offered to sponsor one person from her family to travel to America. Lottie's father had disappeared. Her mother and brother were the only other family. The brother had some health problems, so it was decided that Lottie would be the one to make the trip and start a new life away from the worsening situation in Europe. Although her future husband was able to later join her in the United States, Lottie made the ocean voyage all alone, "with only $2.50 in my pocket," she recalls. She also had her mother's good china and table linens in two trunks.

In New York, Lottie made repeated efforts to bring over her mother and brother who were still in Germany. She did not succeed; both were interned and killed in concentration camps.

Later in life, Lottie worked for many years as a commercial artist. She and her husband never had children and they divorced. As she grew older, she lived alone in a small apartment in Washington, D. C., surrounded by her belongings. She did some reading, she fed neighborhood cats in the alley. Eventually severe arthritis and other health problems limited her mobility and she became dependent on the assistance of neighbors who visited regularly and arranged for Meals on Wheels.

Problems arose when Lottie, still mentally sharp and alert, stubbornly refused more help. Two concerned neighbors, young professional women, became alarmed as Lottie grew weaker and incontinent, but refused hospitalization. When presented with the fact that she couldn't go on living there, Lottie screamed about her freedom and dignity, even though she was barely able to get up from the bed, lying on soiled towels in an old hospital gown held together by clothespins. The mistrust of others and of the unknown she displayed and the need to be in control (or maintain a facade of control) are two characteristics that have been frequently found in Holocaust survivors (Trachtenberg and Davis, 1978; Steinitz, 1984). Finally she was taken by ambulance to a hospital where she was treated for a prolapsed rectum and uterus, dehydration and malnutrition.

In the hospital, Lottie refused to consider the recommendation of entering a nursing home. She returned to her apartment and again deteriorated physically. The two women began court proceedings through which Lottie was declared incompetent to manage her own health care decisions. The two young neighbors were appointed guardian and financial conservator over Lottie. They again had her hospitalized and then admitted to the Hebrew Home.

Staff at the nursing home were aware that Lottie was cognitively intact and had been brought there against her will. They tried to be particularly accommodating, but there were still many problems. Lottie insisted over and over again that she wished to return home. She displayed flashes of paranoia and grandiosity, and a gross lack of understanding of her own limitations. She denied that she had been in terrible condition at home, minimizing her health problems. She raged at her guardians when they visited. They were "double-crossers" who were "drunk with their own power," given by the court. When asked to comply with nursing home routine, she screamed and insisted she would do as she wished. She dramatically reported being "treated like a prisoner" or "a dog," phrases that struck the social worker as especially poignant in light of Lottie's losses in the Holocaust.

Probably the multiple traumas of failing health, loss of independence, and loss of her apartment brought back feelings from the time in her life when Lottie had helplessly learned that her family had been killed by the Nazis. Control and lack of it were major issues for her in the nursing home. Staff learned that on some matters they simply would have to let Lottie win her own way. As an example, they tried for weeks to get her to allow them to remove a large sack of papers from the foot of her bed at night. Each night, Lottie railed and cried and screamed till the staff gave up. Eventually they realized it was not such a necessity for their work after all, and they made the small effort to remove the sack and replace it when they changed the bedding, giving Lottie the comfort and security of keeping her "important papers" near her. In other matters where staff felt they had to have their way, it was found that giving her a choice was helpful. She would say on her scheduled shower day, "Not today." The nursing staff would stand firm that it was to be today but Lottie could choose to have it now or in an hour.

Lottie was deeply angry about having her apartment and its contents given up or sold without her absolute control over the process. Learning about Lottie's experience of coming to America, she being the family's most precious possession, with their other most precious possessions in her two trunks, it is easy to appreciate her strong attachment to those things (and her investment in her own life and independence), bestowed on her by the mother she lost. The social worker worked with the guardian and conservator as well as with Lottie to allow her some reasonable part in decisions regarding her furniture and valuables. Over time, Lottie was able to become somewhat more reasonable and also made a major concession to a future at the Hebrew Home when she requested that a favorite table and her dresser be brought in to her room there.

Another issue, more difficult to resolve, is money. Even when Lottie began gradually to accept that she may need to stay in a nursing home indefinitely, the fact that the court had given her money to the conservator to manage upset her terribly. She confided in the social worker that she had spent her entire life pinching pennies, "denying myself everything" so that she would never be a pauper. We see here possibly a masochistic survivor's guilt (Carmelly, 1975) whereby Lottie punished her own survival by living very simply and frugally. But beyond that, she had saved money so that she would never again be at the mercy of others as her family had been in 1930s Germany. She agonized that her life's savings were rapidly being drained at the nursing home and found little solace in staff's reassurance that, "after the money is gone, you'll be covered by Medicaid." She worried that the government might stop funding that program at any time and that she and all the other old people would be set out in the streets. To someone who has lived through the devastation of the Holocaust years, it is not impossible for governments to betray in unthinkable ways.

Listening and validating Lottie's feelings were the best and probably only courses of action to help her with these concerns. She talked about leaving the nursing home, finding somewhere cheaper to live, getting an apartment again, but her frailty and problems with incontinence made these options untenable. Staff have begun to argue these things with her less and to allow her to express herself more. Through this process Lottie is becoming gradually calmer and more secure in her surroundings at the Hebrew Home.

Bessie: "I know. Leave me alone."

Bessie was born in Holland, the younger of two daughters. When she was a young girl, her mother died and her father re-married. Very strong-willed, Bessie did not get along with her stepmother, especially in food related matters. Her father was a tradesman and the family was comfortable financially. When the Nazis invaded, Bessie's father, in a body cast due to an accident, could not escape and was killed. Her stepmother tried to bribe her way out, but was killed. The sister, who did not look Jewish, brazenly lived in the community. Bessie survived the war by hiding in a succession of attics and working as a domestic with false papers.

Bessie and her husband met, married, and had one son in Europe, after the war. The family came to New York City in 1952. They moved six times to other cities, finally settling in one place in 1965, when she was diagnosed as having multiple sclerosis. Twenty years later, she entered a nursing home, was unhappy there, moved to another facility and then moved to the Hebrew Home in 1990, to be nearer her son and his family. She was 69 years old.

Illness and institutionalization bring out feelings of helplessness and powerlessness (Rosenbloom, 1983) and Bessie *was* completely physically helpless. She required total care with transfers, body positioning, all activities of daily living except for eating. She was mentally alert, with a high mental status exam score. Although she was able to propel her own wheelchair, she rarely attended activities; she was impatient and demanding of staff. She knew exactly when her schedule called for turning and became angry when staff did not respond on the dot. When her husband was visiting, he would wheel her out of her room and they would both seek out her nursing assistant an hour before Bessie's naptime to make certain the schedule was adhered to.

Bessie made one friend on the unit. Particularly vulnerable to loss and separation (Steinitz, 1984; Rosenbloom, 1983), when her friend moved to a unit in our other building, Bessie withdrew and isolated herself even more. She refused to accept visits from volunteers, to meet with social work students, or with her unit social worker. She also refused psychiatric consults. Emotional detachment, which may once have been functional and adaptive now turned pathological (Rosenbloom, 1983).

Bessie's diagnoses included severe GI disease with esophagitis, and GI bleeding. She had sharp epigastric pain, but refused all medications except one. Her weight and appetite both decreased; over a period of six months, she ate less and less, and increasingly refused to get out of bed. The one remaining medication was determined to be contributing to these depressive symptoms, as well as causing severe tardive dyskinetic movements of her face, lips, and tongue, but she refused to allow it to be discontinued. Eventually, her entire upper body was involved in these dystonic movements, but Bessie refused muscle relaxants.

Bessie continued to refuse to eat or to get out of bed. The physician explained that remaining in bed could lead to skin breakdown, that lying down all the time was directly related to her nausea and esophagitis. As nursing staff also tried to emphasize cause and effect, Bessie's anxiety and twitching increased considerably. She said, "I know. Leave me alone."

During this time, Bessie's husband became increasingly angry at his (and the staff's) inability to convince his wife to "listen to reason" and do what he wanted her to do. He was able to acknowledge that he could not keep himself from pushing her to do things his way, and that not being able to control her was very frustrating.

The unit team, the physician, nurse manager, and social worker met with one of the Home's physician/ethicists to discuss the ethical issues involved in Bessie's determination to control her own life. It was decided that she was capable of making her own decisions and should be allowed to do so. Another meeting was held with Bessie, her husband, the physician, nurse manager, and social worker to discuss Bessie's wish to remain in bed and be left alone. The staff assured her that the decision was hers to make, but the team wanted to make sure she understood that she was at increased risk for developing respiratory complications, perhaps even pneumonia, by staying in bed, and that it also exacerbated her chronic esophagitis. She would die if she continued to refuse to eat. Bessie requested that she be turned every two hours, even awakened if asleep, to be turned. She stated that she would not accept a feeding tube under any circumstances.

Bessie continued to refuse all medications except the one she had rigidly insisted upon keeping; she continued to refuse to get out of bed; she would not eat or take any supplements. Her husband continued to ask her to eat and to take her medications. Shortly before she died, still alert, she stated that she did not want to go to the hospital and that she did not want IV treatment. Her husband reluctantly accepted her decision.

During the Holocaust, the Nazis decided who would live or die—and when (Rosenbloom, 1983). But in her later years, Bessie's strong will, reinforced no doubt by what she suffered during the war years, prevailed. Bessie controlled her own life to the very end.

Lena: "I was afraid it might be cancer."

Lena was only seven years old and a polio survivor when the Nazis invaded Poland. In the nursing home, she verbalized very little about her life prior to coming to the United States. Admitting to being a Holocaust survivor, she said she spent the war years in Germany in a sort of Jewish community, but more than this she would not reveal; the community she referred to was probably the concentration camp where her sister and parents were also interned. Lena never answered any questions about this time, explaining that she simply couldn't discuss it because it was too painful. By controlling conversations about her past Lena was able to avoid uncovering unpleasant memories. Like many Holocaust survivors, Lena may have had amnesia for her trauma (Steinitz, 1984) or she may have had the common reaction of being unable to discuss her past because the horror could never be communicated to a nonsurvivor (Conrad, 1969).

When she was 17, Lena and her family came to New York and at 21 she married. She never worked and always depended on her husband's income. Soon after the marriage, Lena's husband lost his job due to physical problems and from then on they depended on his brother's charity for their existence. Lena's pattern of dependence on others for survival was well established by the time she came to the Hebrew Home. First she depended on her parents, then the Nazis, followed by her brother-in-law, and lastly the Home.

Lena and her husband lived together for thirty years, most of the time in a subsidized independent living apartment building built and supervised by the Jewish community. The living arrangement provided the couple with one meal a day; they were to prepare the other two meals in their apartment. The facility's social worker described the couple as antagonistic toward one another. Lena refused to do much, leaving her husband with most of the responsibilities. She isolated herself, apparently rarely leaving the apartment, except for the one meal. She even ignored her health care, never going to a medical or dental appointment. Her husband verbally attacked her for her reclusive behavior.

After thirty years of marriage Lena's husband left her and moved to another apartment in the same building. At this point she stopped going to the dining room and depended on building staff to bring her food. When this behavior continued the social worker became alarmed and went to visit her. She found that Lena had not kept up with her hygiene, nor had she cleaned the apartment since her husband left. Adult Protective Services was called in to assess the situation. They felt she was severely depressed and should be hospitalized. After weeks of discussion and an eviction notice she finally agreed to admit herself. There, a large lump was discovered in Lena's left breast. When asked if she had ever felt it, she said, "Yes, I've had it a long time, but I was afraid it might be cancer."

For the next ten days Lena refused further examination for fear of the diagnosis. Psychiatrists spent time with her trying to convince her that a workup was needed. She was described as suspicious, paranoid, depressed, and sometimes loosely associated. She feared that a physical exam would result in surgery. The psychiatrist surmised that this is what happened to her as a child in the camp; experimental surgery was often done on children with handicaps, and polio had left Lena with a limp.

Lena was diagnosed with metastatic breast cancer and promptly refused treatment, saying that she would pray and hope it would disappear. It became evident that she was in a battle with the doctors for control of her body and was disturbed by their unwillingness to collude with her delusional belief that the cancer would go away on its own. Several doctors spent 45 minutes each with her trying to convince her to undergo surgery. She was only able to express fear of pain and an operation. Eventually she did give in to a mastectomy but refused chemotherapy or further treatment because it would make her feel sick.

Looking much older than her 59 years, Lena was admitted to the Hebrew Home where the staff was told that she had from 4-6 months to live. She had refused further medical intervention, opting to continue her wishful thinking. Moving to the Home was difficult for Lena, who for years had lived in the adjacent building. She said, "I didn't want to come here because people are always going out in ambulances to die." The denial of her illness and the health facade take on special meaning when we consider that disease meant an instant death sentence in the camps (Rosenbloom, 1983).

The Hebrew Home staff worked together to develop a supportive care plan that would give Lena the best quality of life and dignity in her final months. Since she could not tolerate any discussion of her illness or her past, the decision was made to work only on the here and now issues and avoid discussion of her health. The approach to her care was continually revised and discussed as she exhibited new behaviors.

The social worker helped Lena unpack her belongings on the first day because Lena was deeply concerned that someone might steal something. She had already split the staff into good and bad based on religion. The team decided to handle this with reassuring phrases about how much they like Jewish people. It was evident immediately that she had a habit of hoarding undergarments; she began to complain of needing more as 42 slips and 100 pair of stockings were unpacked. Confronting Lena with the actual number of items in her drawers seemed to reduce the times she requested more of these items in the weeks that followed.

During the first weeks Lena enjoyed participating in activities, but she rapidly became more paranoid and suspicious of other residents. She would refuse to go into the activity room for fear that someone might hurt her. The staff tried to reassure her but she chose to withdraw from social activities rather than risk being involved in an unknown. She began to sit in front of the nursing station all day. This was difficult for staff who found her constant questions distracting and irritating. The team decided to give a uniform, acceptable, and non-rejecting response to her. The consistency helped Lena find some predictability and stability in her life. It also prevented her from further splitting the staff into good and bad components, creating more trust for Lena.

Shower days and doctors rounds were also power struggles, partly because of the disturbance in her normal routine and partly because of past experiences and their significance. The team tried to reduce her perception of the Home as an institution of blind conformity by giving her some responsibility in decision making. Staff offered her different times to choose from for showers and the physician gave her the option of seeing him now or in an hour. This did very little to reduce her anxiety about having to have a shower or see a doctor, but it did offer her some control over her care.

As Lena's health deteriorated her trust and appreciation of staff grew. She developed a special relationship with her primary nursing assistant who spent greater time with Lena putting on makeup and doing her hair. She went out to lunch with the activities therapist for her birthday and asked the social worker to go on a trip to Florida with her in the future when she felt better. In the final week of Lena's life the entire staff took turns feeding and talking to her. She was not unhappy or in pain. Victimization continued through Lena's life, first as a survivor of polio, then as a survivor of a concentration camp, followed by a long torturous marriage which she didn't feel empowered to leave, and finally by the cancer which was too frightening for her to fight. Although she never accepted the gravity of her illness or understood that she might possibly have overcome it, Lena's last months were spent among caregivers who provided her with a safe and accepting environment. She was able to maintain some control over her situation and make some connections to others while receiving the care she needed.

Jack: "We must be very careful."

Jack is a Hebrew Home resident who has lived on several different units during his time here, reflecting an interest in finding a reasonable placement for him, as well as for those who live in proximity to him. This is a gentleman whose life was ruined by the Nazis as surely as though he had gone to the gas chambers.

Although Jack himself is no longer a reliable informant, from his son and ex-wife it has been learned that he was treated brutally and inhumanly during the Holocaust. As a young man he hid in a chimney and listened to the murder of his whole family. Later he hid in haystacks for months on end, living on scraps left by a sympathetic farmer. Before the war ended Jack had escaped from three different concentration camps. He learned, by age 35, how to run, hide, and survive.

Even in the U.S., life was not easy for him. According to his family he was unsuccessful in his business, losing it due to his inability to trust his partner. He was also unsuccessful at marriage. The "sense that people are not trustworthy" (Steinitz, 1984, p. 335) has surely impeded his success with human relationships throughout his life.

Then came old age! After Jack needed more care than the adjacent senior apartment building could provide, Jack was admitted to the Hebrew Home in February 1991. His diagnoses include: Parkinson's disease, depression, pseudo bulbar palsey, diabetes mellitus, arteriosclerotic heart disease, a history of hepatic cirrhosis, and dementia with delusional psychosis. In less than two years he has lived unsuccessfully on at least four units. He has been described as "verbally aggressive" and "sexually inappropriate."

During the past four years a psychiatrist from the nearby community has been involved periodically. This psychiatrist is called upon when management and medication issues become especially complicated. He describes Jack as having Axis I and Axis II problems (per DSM-III classification), representing the view that describing behavior is valid and helpful regardless of how and why that behavior developed. There are Axis I diagnoses that encompass episodes of paranoia and serious depression, sometimes occurring together; there are also Axis II personality problems that predispose Jack to self-centeredness, inappropriate secretiveness, sexual provocativeness, and tranquilizer-seeking behavior.

In addition to psychiatric consultation as needed, the consideration of interventions is limited by Jack's substantial cognitive losses. It falls to the social worker to be knowledgeably supportive of his inner turmoil even though it is not possible to engage him in any insight-oriented kind of counseling. Armed with background knowledge, however, staff can try to make the atmosphere as non-threatening as possible. Creating opportunities for Jack to have control (e.g. shower time, food preferences) seems important, as does providing a maximum number of occasions for calm and nurturing support. On one unit baths instead of showers helped until gradual adjustment to showers was attained. On another unit Jack seemed comforted by the voice of a German-speaking nurse.

It is futile to attempt to answer whether Jack had any reasonable chance of developing differently than he did given the overwhelming trauma of his early manhood. What we do see is him calling aside the social worker after lunch one memorable afternoon. He calls her to his room so he cannot be overheard. Then he tells her he knows she is a Jew, which is why he must warn her. The nursing aide who served him lunch (a black Jamaican woman) is described as a Nazi who wants to kill us. "We must be very careful," he cautions.

CONCLUSION

The five residents described here, each with his or her own drama and multiple tragedies, point to the essential importance of understanding every individual within the context of his own life history. The social worker, traditionally appointed the gatherer and processor of psychosocial material, is in a unique position to understand these histories, interpret and share them with the other team members and, most important, find ways to use that knowledge for the development of creative and effective treatment plans. As mental health caregivers, we soon realize we cannot "cure," in any substantial way, the abnormal or dysfunctional deep-seated patterns we observe. However, we can use our clinical social work skills, combined with a knowledge of our residents' particular historical experiences, to best advantage when we can make our own institution as warm, accepting, and flexible as is possible. This should be our goal for all nursing home residents, but the need is especially compelling when the resident's only other institutional experience for self or close family members has been a concentration camp.

As we see from Dora, Lottie, Bessie, Lena, and Jack, the level of cognition remaining has great bearing on the specific interventions possible. All five exhibited significant fear, resistance, and paranoia when faced with moderate to total dependence on others for their nursing care. While Bessie, in the end, took total charge of her final decisions and days, Jack will not have the mental capacity to have such a level of self-determination. However, we have shown that there are myriad ways we can work to gain the trust and maximize the sense of personal control of those who at a previous time were totally and cruelly controlled by others. Here at the Home we emphasize patient and understanding listening, the offer of choices wherever and as much as humanly possible, careful attention to placement and roommates, psychiatric intervention as needed, appropriate staff education, and truly making our actions speak louder than our words about patient self-determination where medical treatments are concerned. All these strategies can contribute to making our survivors' last days as good as they can be.

REFERENCES

American Psychiatric Association (1987). *Diagnostic and Statistical Manual of Mental Disorders.* Washington, D.C.: Author.

Blumenfeld, S. (1982). The hospital center and aging: A challenge for the social worker. *Journal of Gerontological Social Work, 5*(1/2), 44-46.

Bowsher, J. E., & Gerlach, M. J. (1990). Personal control and other determinants of psychological well-being in nursing home elders. *Scholarly Inquiry for Nursing Practice: An International Journal, 4*(2), 91-102.

Burr, H. T. (1986). The patient as hero: A psychotherapeutic approach to work with resistant aged patients. *Clinical Gerontologist, 6*(2), 13-16.

Carmelly, F. (1975). Guilt feelings in concentration camp survivors: Comments of a "survivor." *Journal of Jewish Communal Service, 75,* 139-144.

Conrad, G. (1969). Casework with survivors of Nazi persecution twenty years after liberation. *Journal of Jewish Communal Service, 7,* 170-175.

Harel, Z. & Kahana, E. (1988). Psychosocial well-being among Holocaust survivors and immigrants in Israel. *Journal of Traumatic Stress, 3*(4), 413-429.

Hertz, D. G. (1990). Trauma and nostalgia: New aspects on the coping of aging Holocaust survivors. *Israeli Journal of Psychiatry and Related Sciences, 27*(4), 189-198.

Kuch, K., & Cox, B. J. (1992, March). Symptoms of PTSD in 124 survivors of the Holocaust. *American Journal of Psychiatry, 149*(3), 337-339.

Meunier, G. F. & Schulz, K. (1991). Brief therapy for an adjustment disorder precipitated by admission to a nursing home. *Clinical Gerontologist, 11*(1), 73-76.

Raber, W. C., Lamboo, F., Mitchell-Pederson, L. (1986). From duckling to swan. *Clinical Gerontologist,* 6(2), 179-188.

Robinson, S., Rapaport, J., Durst, R., Rapaport, M., Rosca, P., Metzer, S., Zilberman, L. (1990). The late effects of Nazi persecution among elderly Holocaust survivors. *Acta Psychiatr Scand, 82,* 311-315.

Rosenbloom, M. (1983, April). Implications of the Holocaust for social work. *Social Casework: The Journal of Contemporary Social Work,* 205-213.

Segal, J. (1986). *Winning Life's Toughest Battles.* New York: MacGraw-Hill.

Steinitz, L.Y. (1984). Psychosocial effects of the Holocaust on aging survivors and their families. *Journal of Jewish Communal Service, 60*(4), 331-336.

Trachtenberg, M. & Davis, M. (1978). Breaking silence: Serving children of Holocaust survivors. *Journal of Jewish Communal Service, 54,* 294-302.

Zarit, S. H., Zarit, J. M., and Rosenberg-Thompson, S. (1990). A special treatment unit for Alzheimer's disease: Medical, behavioral, and environmental features. *Clinical Gerontologist, 9*(3/4), 47-63.

Bonding and Separateness, Two Major Factors in the Relations Between Holocaust Survivors and Their Children

Dina Wardi, MSW

EDITOR'S INTRODUCTION TO THE CHAPTER: The relationship of the mental health of the aging and intergenerational relations has been a major topic in *Clinical Gerontologist* over the years. Wardi uses a psychoanalytic perspective to examine the impact of the Holocaust on intergenerational relations. The ideal situation is a balance between closeness and separation. The boundaries of the parent-child relationship (and what I would call "appropriate role expectations") are challenged by the Holocaust experience, as well as by the process of aging. Wardi then presents examples of therapy for the next generation.

Many Holocaust survivors have by now reached old age. Some have already died, while others are facing death. Their sons and daughters who have already reached maturity, many of them parents to grown up children themselves, are accompanying their parents through this universally complex and painful stage. In this chapter I want to deal with the specific, and perhaps somewhat unique, patterns of behaviour and emotional reactions which reflect some of the conflictual areas in the intergenerational transmission between survivors and their children.

[Haworth co-indexing entry note]: "Bonding and Separateness, Two Major Factors in the Relations Between Holocaust Survivors and Their Children." Wardi, Dina. Co-published simultaneously in the *Clinical Gerontologist* (The Haworth Press, Inc.) Vol. 14, No. 3, 1994, pp. 119-131; and: *Holocaust Survivors' Mental Health* (ed: T. L. Brink) The Haworth Press, Inc., 1994, pp. 119-131. Multiple copies of this article/chapter may be purchased from The Haworth Document Delivery Center [1-800-3-HA-WORTH; 9:00 a.m. - 5:00 p.m. (EST)].

119

The experience of loss and separation accompanies us throughout our lives, in essence from birth until the moment of death; that is to say that the life experience creates within itself the integral experience of separation which in turn has within it as a crucial aspect the ability to cut off and release a major portion of the libidinal feelings and urges concentrated in one person, and to invest them in another person and in a new life situation (A. Freud, 1967).

The ability to pass through life's stages from birth through adolescence and maturity into old age and death in a natural and relatively easy manner derives from one's internal ability to experience separation in an optimal manner, as conflict free as possible.

It is safe to assume that for survivors who experienced the personal and collective trauma in whose center stands total, brutal loss, the ability to experience separation and to pass from one life stage to another is especially difficult and filled with conflict, especially since within this experience of trauma and loss is thrust the additional trauma of the inability to experience mourning and separation (H. Klein, 1973; Mitscherlich, 1979).

The survivors, finding themselves after the war, in a vacuum, completely isolated physically after years of exposure to methodical acts of dehumanization and destruction of their personal and collective identity, had no place to mourn, no grave and no monument. Nor did they have any internal opportunity to mourn; in fact, the opposite was true: Those survivors who were already adults during the Holocaust years, after completing the various processes of separation and individuation, often returned to their earlier developmental stages and linked up with their internalized objects or partial objects, through a sharp process of inner fragmentation (J. S. Kestenberg, 1972). The attachment and merging with innerdirected objects (other parental and spousal figures) through massive use of defenses such as repression and emotional isolation, helped them maintain their inner core that allowed their fragile and vulnerable selves to maintain a certain balance (Wardi, 1992).

The process of grief and mourning was impossible, as it depended on facing such a huge amount of pain and loneliness that it was usually avoided altogether, bringing with it the possibility of such an emotional flood that threatened the complete dissolution of one's self. The bulk of the libido (urges + emotions) thus remained involved in the internalized lost objects, including mother, father, close sibling, or even a small baby who was killed, such that any remaining emotional energies available for investment in a spousal or, later, a parent-child relationship, were extremely limited (Lipkowitz, 1973; Rakoff, 1969).

If we return now to children born after the Holocaust, we know that they represented the most precious thing for their parents, and that they represented the reason for, and significance of their parents' lives, and even a symbol of their victory over the Nazis through their survival.

While the baby is still in his survivor mother's womb, his presence becomes a temporary means of dissipating her constant feeling of lonely existence. At the same time, the fetus becomes an integral part of its mother who molds with it completely, with no boundaries separating them, and with the child totally safe and protected from any dangers or threats that exist in the outer, hostile world.

But at the end of the pregnancy comes birth, and it is then that the survivor mother must deal with the difficult experience of separation, a deep wound still affecting her self identity and self evaluation, even injuring her as yet healthy narcissism. She is unable to deal with yet another injury to her narcissism, just as she is unable to deal with another act of separation. In her inner world, every act of separation is interpreted as a final, absolute loss, something inherently associated with death, disappearance and abandonment.

The constant fear of existence which pounds mournfully within her, evokes patterns of survival in their sharpest forms, those patterns of maximum control over one's environment and over her baby. The ultimate purpose is to protect the baby's life at any cost, with her permanent sense of over-protection from which she feeds the baby, guards its health and takes care that it not leave her sight (Wardi, 1992).

This situation does not allow the mother to identify and deal with her baby's needs, especially his emotional ones, when dealing with his independent and separate needs, and primarily his need for separateness in order to learn to take control of his own helplessness and protect his 'selfness.' Here especially one sees the survivor mother's difficulty in ridding herself of feelings of isolation, depression and guilt that fill her inner being, and in seeing the child itself and not solely as a continuation of the dead images internalized in her world; thus, many members of the second generation become 'memorial candles' to parents and their families, carrying with them unconscious aspects identifying themselves with these dead objects (Sigal, 1971; Kestenberg, 1972, 1982; Gumpel, 1982).

As these children mature, many second generation children find it difficult to experience the natural processes of rebellion and of separateness and individuation. The ability to rebel in survivor families comes up against many difficulties, not least of which is the ability to express the usual adolescent anger or aggression against their parents, accompanied by strong feelings of guilt. The boundaries of anger and aggression are very unclear and there is a fear of losing control in these situations.

We must also remember, though, that with every expression of separation and separateness on the part of the adolescent, the parents usually react with anxiety and rage; after all, for the parent survivor, the son or daughter is the continuation of and replacement for the family members who were killed, even to the point being named after them, and thus the child also shares in the parent's inner world and carries with him the burden of death, pain and loss.

It is primarily from those children chosen to act as 'memorial candles' (Wardi, 1992) that separation is especially difficult. This convergence does not, of course, help those second generation members who are growing up, to easily deal with the process of their inner separation and does not allow or at least makes more difficult the possibility of establishing a separate, independent identity.

As a child of the second generation grows up, reaching the stage where he leaves home and separates (at least physically) from his parents, devoting his energies to building an independent life of his own, here too is experienced a separation from one stage and passage into a new stage of life, something that demands the release of emotional energies from the thrall of the parents, to be invested in the establishment of a newly shared life (Zwerling, 1982).

Here we witness once again the renewed attention to that central and conflicting aspect of dealing with both convergence and separateness, the cornerstone in building a contiguous, shared and intimate relationship; in dealing with his sexuality and sense of sharing, the ability to separate from the internalized parent and create a shared relationship that contains an appropriate balance which is mutually satisfying for both partners within the aspects of attachment and separation, while maintaining and respecting each other's boundaries.

A portion of second generation members never succeed in maintaining a long term relationship and they resolve this conflict by getting involved only in temporary and impossible relationships which do not demand any investment or deep attachment and thus avoid dealing in the long term with the difficulty in achieving a balance between closeness and separateness (Wardi, 1992).

Another group of second generation members does, indeed, succeed in establishing long term relationships, in marrying and having children of their own; however, there too is often found a difficulty with convergence separation appearing in varying degrees and in different variations. Their functioning level is seen primarily in the area of 'doing,' both in their professional skills and in their ability to run a household, care for their children indicate that they are sharing responsibilities and functioning normally. However, on a more intimate level of sharing separation, we frequently find difficulties reflected in aspects of intimacy, which is usually extremely limited, and in patterns of dependence and control which appear quite frequently.

The maturing second generation member also often finds himself in conflict with a feeling of dual loyalties between his parents on the one hand and his partner and children on the other. The boundaries become more and more unclear and it becomes more difficult to maintain them, with the result being that the young family finds it difficult to maintain a semblance of internal and external separateness appropriate for them and their nuclear family.

Another separation aspect that second generation members must deal with during this period of their lives is the confrontation with old age and with their parents' decisions and preparations for death, as well as the final separation from them.

The aging of a large number of Holocaust survivors is accompanied by the usual effects of the aging process: Weakening of one's physical powers and decreasing ability to function independently, often combined with a weakening of the mental defense system that existed for so many years. The regressive mental process that occurs in this stage often raises the need to reconnect with one's distant past along with a smaller emotional investment in the present.

Survivors who had buried and repressed the past over decades, now find themselves in a position with less control and with a greater need to return to those times and talk about them, despite the difficulties and threats this might entail.

This process is accelerated by the increasing openness and legitimacy within the Israeli society as a whole and among the grandchildren, growing older, who often provide the incentive and release for the grandparents, since the grandchildren have the ability to confront their grandfathers and grandmothers and ask them about their pasts in a direct and open manner. The desire and need of the third generation to know and to connect emotionally to history and to the continuity of their truncated family are accepted by the grandparents without the feeling of tension and threat that accompanied the questions of the second generation; the aging survivors feel that they are running out of time, a feeling that makes them want even more to tell their story, to provide their testimonies, to leave a real memorial to the family that perished.

The parent survivor, caught by his child throughout his life between the duality of helpless victim on the one hand and mythic, omnipotent figure on the other, becomes now, in reality, the weaker one, in need of spiritual and physical support. In this situation, where it is often necessary to become a parent to one's parent, the child must again deal not only with role reversal but with the intimacy and closeness the situation demands, with aspects of convergence and separateness again coming sharply into play.

Here too we can identify two extreme patterns on one axis: At one end we find second generation members totally devoted to caring for their sick and elderly parent. Here we see a renewed, total convergence without the ability to preserve one's personal boundaries, with an imbalanced emotional investment between one's partner and one's parent. In these instances there is a conscious and often unconscious fear of separation and the approaching death.

We must remember that in many cases, despite the fact that second generation members were surrounded by death from the moment of their birth, they had never experienced the actual death of a relative, i.e., grandparent, etc., since there was, indeed, no family . . . Often, the feelings that arise in these situations are so sharp and threatening, that the second generation member defends himself by totally cutting himself off emotionally, and thus returning to using patterns of control and to functional 'doing.' In these patterns, second generation members will act automatically, unable to connect to any stronger or more significant feelings during the remainder of this stage.

A combination of feelings of anger and guilt may arise once again in full force, expressed either directly or indirectly. When the "I" does not separate on the internal level and the second generation member's identity is not yet fully integrated, a particular difficulty will appear at this point: The ability to devote oneself to and care for the parent on an intimate level and to experience a pleasant feeling of "together," is usually impossible if it had not occurred previously in the course of one's life. The difficulty in approaching feelings of sadness, pain, loss and grief will also be great, insofar as the second generation member did not previously experience emotionally any feelings of the total loss that his parents had experienced in the Holocaust, and did not succeed in meeting and working out the pain on some level, mourning for those losses.

If the second generation member did, in fact, go through the working through and release of the heavy weight of the deaths that he had carried all his life in his internal world, he will have a greater chance to deal with the death of his parent, and to grieve for him, to separate from him and to serve as a different example for his own children in this particular, crucial point.

I would like now to bring forth three examples which manifest three different patterns of dealing with bonding and separateness between aging survivors and their grown up children.

I

Hava, a single woman of 42, is the only daughter of two survivor parents. She applied to AMCHA' * for psychotherapeutic help, complaining of anxieties and stress, mentioning that her mother was

---

*The Israeli Center for Psychological Support of Survivors of the Holocaust and the Second Generation.

suffering from cancer and was already in a very serious condition. In her late twenties she had left Israel and had lived since in New York for over ten years, working at several casual employments, and never being able to maintain a permanent relationship with a partner. She feels that all along her stay in New York, she and her parents were reciprocally involved in each other's lives. "Through endless long-distance calls, my mother continued to have control over me and to affect many of my decisions. I tried to cut myself off from them, to run away, but it didn't really work." Clearly, the internal separation had not taken place, not even with the geographical distance. When she heard of her mother's illness, Hava left everything behind, rushed to Israel and settled down in her parents' apartment. From that moment on, she dedicated herself completely to her parent's care, accompanying her mother to hospital for treatment and supporting her eighty year old father, without leaving any space for her own life. In the last phase, when the mother was hospitalized, Hava hardly ever left her bedside. At times she found herself lying in her mother's hospital bed.

It seems quite clear that Hava was flooded with separation anxiety and had regressed into a state where she was completely merged with her mother, both physically and emotionally, all the boundaries between them having been removed. After the mother's death, Hava did not manifest sorrow or mourning. Neither crying nor any other expression of grief could be observed in her countenance. It looked as if she had worn a frozen mask. As time went by, she seemingly returned to regular life and even took some sort of employment. However she very often wore her dead mother's clothes and went on living with her aged father, taking upon herself the role previously fulfilled by her mother. Apparently she embodied in some way her mother's identity and was not able to separate from her internalized self-object parts. Her emotional detachment and isolation became more and more pronounced, her defences grew more rigid, and shortly after she broke up her therapy.

Through the unconscious mechanism of transposition, Hava had internalized the projected self-object parts of both parents, containing massive loss and death. Her two parents lost not only the totality of their larger families, but also former spouses and infant children, whose identities remained fixated in their internal worlds.

Through a mechanism of projection identification these identities were eventually projected upon Hava from her earliest infancy. As a result her own identity came to include fragments of a multitude of dead objects, and hence remained confused and totally fragmented. The arduous process of separation and individuation turned out apparently to be a task too exacting for her fragile self and her limited inner resources. Indeed, so extensive was that portion of her soul that it had unconsciously become merged with her parents' souls, in the world of the past, sometime, somewhere, even before the black abyss of the Holocaust.

II

Ruth, aged 45, married and mother of two children, is the daughter of a survivor mother. She lives in a kibbutz and her duty is to attend to the needs of the elderly kibbutz members. She says that she likes her work and derives much satisfaction from it. She enjoys the possibility to impart empathy and warmth to these old men and women, while ministering to their physical and emotional needs. On the other hand, her visits to her own widowed mother, living by herself in a far removed town, were until recently very infrequent, and seem to have caused Ruth great frustration and anxiety. Lately the mother has come to live in the same place as her daughter, and naturally they started seeing each other much more frequently. This, however did not improve the situation much, as the mother has now become bitterly jealous of the other old people her daughter was attending to. Ruth says: "I feel that I can't come close to her, neither physically nor emotionally, and her having come to live nearby only makes it more tense and difficult for me."

Some time ago Ruth joined an AMCHA second generation therapeutic group, and with its assistance she managed, in a first phase, to make contact with the anger and guilt that she had felt towards her mother, and work through them. She also dared to face some of the indescribable traumas experienced by her mother as a young girl in the Holocaust. Some other group members followed suit, and together they worked through this difficult phase, in which the members share much pain and anxiety. In other words, Ruth and her mates mourned together for the multiple deaths and massive losses, to which they have been exposed along with their parents.

In the next phase, Ruth learned to accept her mother's emotional limitations, derived from the painful internal injuries inflicted upon her young soul by massive loss and trauma, and to acknowledge her long concealed old yearning for a close and warm relation with her mother.

Toward the end of the group process Ruth stated that she was feeling a marked change in her relations with her mother. "I can talk to her now in a different way. I feel much less tense and irritable. I am more patient with her and at times I even feel warmth for her."

To a certain extent, Ruth has undoubtedly succeeded to disengage her own self from her mother's internalized identity, or, more specifically, from that introjected self-object part, so totally imbued with death, loss, guilt and anger. It is this separation that now becomes evident in her new ability to feel empathy towards her old survivor mother.

III

A couple of parents, Yossi and Yael, are second generation members in their 40s. They have three children, ages 5, 12 and 16. They are both very successful professionals, he in business, and she in the arts. The family lives in an orderly apartment and has an active social life, on the surface appearing as a typical, successful Israeli family.

The children themselves can also be described as successful, except for the middle child, Yair, who has been experiencing learning difficulties but is nonetheless described as a child with a very well developed, creative imagination, who devotes a great deal of his time to dancing in a youth dance troupe and in writing stories.

Yael, the mother, is in treatment with me. She began therapy as a result of several problems and a feeling of distress within the relationship. She described the main pattern between her and Yossi as one of control and dependence and as a result she felt depressed and unfulfilled. She also repeatedly mentioned the feeling that something was missing in the intimate dialogue between her and her husband, that there was some sort of confinement there, and she felt that her husband was cut off and closed emotionally.

The husband, not in treatment, denies the situation and claims that he does not see any problems or difficulties in his relationship with his wife, nor does he understand what is troubling her. Yossi's father, an 87 year old survivor widowed many years previously, had died a few months earlier. Yael describes her father-in-law as a difficult, closed man who almost never spoke, and to whom it was very difficult to get close emotionally. He had lived, during the last few years, with his daughter, Yossi's sister, who took him into her home and cared for him devotedly, seeing to all his needs to a degree that seemed to Yael quite excessive. "Many times, I thought," Yael says, "that it was really excessive. My sister-in-law gave her father so much that it was at the expense of her relationship with her husband, which was troublesome in any case, and even at the expense of her relationship with her children. You know, she effectively threw her children out of their room, and gave it to their grandfather, forcing the adolescents to sleep in the living room without even a corner to themselves.

"My husband," she continues to describe, "was quite cut off from all this. He fulfilled his formal, minimal responsibilities, going over there every so often for a short visit, and during the last few years never even inviting his father over to our house, on the pretext that he would not be able to climb the four flights. He was quite distanced from his father, and never really talked to him, not about the past and not about the present. I don't think his father ever told him what really happened. Yossi, however, did know about his three year old sister who had died in the ghetto, after they were forced to abandon her, and about another son, born in the forests after they escaped and joined the partisans, who starved to death . . . "

About two months ago, the father died suddenly at home. Yael describes that when they reached her sister-in-law's and Yossi saw how they were putting his father's body into the Burial Society's van, tears came momentarily to his eyes and it looked as if he might burst into tears, but he quickly controlled himself and his tears.

During the funeral and the week of shiva, Yossi did not express any sadness or grief. Most of the time he seemed cut off emotionally, despite the fact that the one remaining uncle told many stories about the past and the Holocaust. After the shiva, when he returned home, Yossi returned to his previous routine, regaining control over it very quickly.

When I asked Yael whether Yossi or she had talked with the children about their grandfather's death or had displayed any signs of mourning or grief, Yael looked at me at first in astonishment and then, showing a certain degree of sadness, she said, no, but that she felt very uneasy about it and it seemed too bad that neither she nor Yossi were able to pass on enough to the children and to talk to them more about emotional and sensitive things, such as this particular event.

She continued to deal with this matter for a certain period of time and tried to express to Yossi a bit more of her thoughts and feelings.

In one of the sessions during this period, she said that she wanted to read me a story that her son Yair had written in school, that she felt was significant. In the story, Yair went to heaven where he met his grandfather, who asked him to come closer. When Yair came closer and his grandfather hugged and stroked him, it felt very pleasant. He asked his grandfather various questions, and his grandfather talked and talked.

On the eve of Passover soon afterwards, Yair asked that his parents leave an empty chair at the Seder table for grandfather.

Yair, a third generation member, succeeded in his own way to grieve and to preserve the place and memory of his grandfather. Yossi the son did not succeed in grieving for his father, just as he failed to succeed in achieving any sort of dialogue or intimacy with him while he was still alive. But despite this, he succeeded in giving his son Yair the inner space in which his emotional and creative worlds could exist and where Yair could feel and express through his writing his pain over his grandfather's death, even succeeding to correct in his imagination and to fill in what he missed while his grandfather was still alive. The grandfather, who had lost two of his own small children in addition to the rest of his entire extended family, locked up the warmth of his love and could only pass it on to Yair in this very indirect manner.

REFERENCES

Freud, A. and Dann, S. (1951). "An experiment in group upbringing," *Psychoanalytic Study of the Child*, 6, 127-69.

Gumpel, Y. (1982). "A daughter of silence." In M. S. Bergmann & M. E. Jucovy, (Eds), *Generations of the Holocaust*, New York: Basic books. 120–36.

Kestenberg, J. S. (1972). "Psychoanalytic contribution to the problem of children of survivors from Nazi persecution," *Israel annals of Psychiatry and Related Disciplines*, 10, 311-25.

Klein, H. (1973). "Children of the Holocaust: Mourning and bereavement." In E. J. Antony & C. Koupernik (Eds), *The Child in His Family*, 393-409.

Lipkowitz, M. H. (1973). "The child of two survivors: A report of an unsuccessful therapy," *Israeli annals of Psychiatry and Related Disciplines*, 2, 363-74.

Mitscherlich, A. (1979). "Die Notwendigkeit zu Trauern'," In Maerthesheimer (Ed), *Cruezfeuer: Der Fernsehfilm Holocaust*, Maerthesheimer.

Rakoff, v. (1979). "Children and families of concentration camp survivors," *Canada's Mental Health*, 14, 24-6.

Sigal, J. (1971). "Second generation effects of massive trauma," *International Psychiatry Clinics*, 8, 55-65.

Wardi, Dina. (1992). *Memorial Candles: Children of the Holocaust*, Tavistock Routledge, London & New York, 1992.

Zwerling, I. (1982). "A comparison of parent-child attachment and separation in American Holocaust survivor families." Presented at a meeting of the American Mental Health Association for Israel (AMHAI), Chicago.

APPENDIXES

Appendixes:
Hebrew and Yiddish
Translations

EDITOR'S INTRODUCTION TO THE APPENDIXES: Yiddish, Hebrew, Rumanian and Russian versions of the brief (15-item) version of the Geriatric Depression Scale were published in Clinical Gerontologist, 8(2), pages 72-83. Several of the authors whose chapters appear in this volume were asked to do complete translations of the full Geriatric Depression Scale, as well as the Hypochondriasis Scale and International Version of the Mental Status Questionnaire. The Hebrew versions of the IVMSQ, GDS, and Hypochondriasis scale published here were developed by Eli Somer, and the Yiddish versions are by Esther-Lee Marcus and Pesach Lichtenberg and Yehoshua Rochman. The editor will welcome future articles and clinical comments about the validity, reliability, and use of these translations.

[Haworth co-indexing entry note]: "Appendixes: Hebrew and Yiddish Translations." Co-published simultaneously in the *Clinical Gerontologist* (The Haworth Press, Inc.) Vol. 14, No. 3, 1994, pp. 135-142; and: *Holocaust Survivors' Mental Health* (ed: T. L. Brink) The Haworth Press, Inc., 1994, pp. 135-142. Multiple copies of this article/chapter may be purchased from The Haworth Document Delivery Center [1-800-3-HAWORTH; 9:00 a.m. - 5:00 p.m. (EST)].

135

APPENDIX 1 (Hebrew Version)

INTERNATIONAL VERSION OF MENTAL STATUS QUESTIONAIRE

גירסה בינלאומית לשאלון סטטוס מנטלי
עיבוד ותרגום עברי: דר' אלי זומר
(זהו מבחן של סטטוס מנטלי ולא של אורגניות)

1. בן/ת כמה את/ה? (בטווח של שנתיים)

2. באיזו שנה נולדת? (בדיוק)

3. מהי השנה עכשיו? (בדיוק)

4. באיזה חודש אנחנו נמצאים כעת? (בדיוק)

5. איזו היא הארוחה האחרונה שאכלת? ארוחת בוקר? ארוחת צהרים?
   ארוחת ערב?

6. איך קוראים למקום הזה? (שם המקום או תיאורו)

7. ספור/ספרי לאחור כמו שעושים האסטרונאוטים: 10, 9, 8 וכו'.

[לקשישים הגרים בקהילה]

8. מה כתובתך? (שם הרחוב ומספר הבית).

9. איזה יום בשבוע היום?

10. מי הוא הנשיא כיום?
    IN ISRAEL ASK : מי הוא ראש הממשלה כיום? (WHO IS PRIME
    (MINISTER NOW?

[לקשישים בבית אבות]

8. כמה זמן את/ה כבר נמצא במקום הזה? (מותרת סטיה של 20%)

9. מי מנהל את המקום הזה?

10. איך מגיעים מכאן לחדר האוכל?

ציינון = מספר התשובות הנכונות.
בלבול בינוני 6 - 4   בלבול חמור 3 - 0
צלול ועירני 10- 9   בלבול קל 8 - 7

הערה: כאשר הפציינט חי/ה בסביבה שבה אין רמזים היכולים לסייע
בהתמצאות זמן - מרחב, יש להעביר את המבחן פעמיים, כאשר בפעם
הראשונה יש לתת לפציינס את התשובה הנכונה על כל תשובה לא נכונה
הנתנת. אם הפציינט זוכר את התשובה הנכונה בפעם השניה, הרי שהטעות
ההתחלתית לא נבעה מדמנטיה, אלא מתנאי הסביבה.

APPENDIX 1 (Yiddish Version)

INTERNATIONAL VERSION OF MENTAL STATUS QUESTIONNAIRE

‎1. ‏ווי אלט זענט איר ?

‎2. ‏אין וואס פאַר א יאָר זענט איר געבוירען-געוואָרן ?

‎3. ‏וואָס פאַר אַ יאָר איז איצט ?

‎4. ‏וואָס פאַר אַ מאָנאַט (חודש) איז איצט ?

‎(‏אָדער וואָס פאַר אַ תקופה : זומער, ווינטער...)

‎5. ‏וועלעכער סעודה (מאָלצייט) האָט איר געגעסן

‎לעצטנס ? פרישטיק ? מיטאָג ? אָוונטברויט ?

‎6. ‏ווי הייסט דער בנין ?

‎7. ‏ציילט אין אַ פאָקערטן אָרדענונג: פון צען (10) צו איינס (1)

(for community elders)

‎8. ‏וואָס איז אייער אדרעס ?

‎9. ‏וועלעכער טאָג אין די וואָך איז היינט ?

‎10. ‏ווער איז דער פרעזידענט (אָדער פּרעמיער-מיניסטער) איצט ?

(for institutionalized elders)

‎8. ‏וויפל צייט זענט איר דא אין דעם שפּיטאָל ?

‎9. ‏ווער איז דער מנהל (שעף) פון דעם שפּיטאל ?

‎10. ‏ווי אזוי גייט מען צו דעם עס-זאַל ?

APPENDIX 2 (Hebrew Version)

GERIATRIC DEPRESSION SCALE (GDS)

סולם דכאון גריאטרי (ס.ד.ג.)

עיבוד ותרגום עברי: דר' אלי זומר

1. האם את/ה מרוצה מחייך באופן כללי?　ל

2. האם הפסקת להתעניין בפעילויות ובנושאים רבים שעיניינו אותך?　כ

3. האם אתה חש/ה שחייך ריקים?　כ

4. האם את/ה נוטה להשתעמם לעיתים תכופות?　כ

5. האם את/ה חש תקוה לגבי העתיד?　ל

6. האם את/ה מוטרד/ת ממחשבות שאינך יכול/ה להוציא מראשך?　כ

7. האם את/ה במצב רוח טוב רוב הזמן?　ל

8. האם את/ה חושש/ת שמשהו רע עלול לקרות לך?　כ

9. האם את/ה חש/ה מאושר/ת רוב הזמן?　ל

10. האם את/ה חש/ה חסר/ת אונים לעיתים הכופות?　כ

11. האם את/ה חש/ה חסר/ת מנוחה ועצבני/ת לעיתים תכופות?　כ

12. האם את/ה מעדיף/ה להשאר בבית בלילה, במקום לצאת ולעשות דברים חדשים?　כ

13. האם את/ה דואג/ת לגבי העתיד לעיתים תכופות?　כ

14. האם את/ה חש/ה שיש לך יותר בעיות עם הזכרון מאשר לרוב האנשים?　כ

15. האם את/ה חש/ה שזה נהדר להיות בחיים עכשיו?　ל

16. האם את/ה מרגיש/ה לעיתים תכופות עצוב/ה ומדוכדך/ת?　כ

17. האם את/ה מרגיש/ה די חסר/ת ערך כפי שהנך היום?　כ

18. האם את/ה דואג/ת הרבה ביחס לעבר?　כ

19. האם את/ה מוצא/ת שהחיים מלהיבים מאד?　ל

20. האם קשה לך להתחיל בפרויקטים חדשים?　כ

21. האם את/ה חש/ה מלא/ת אנרגיה?　ל

22. האם את/ה חש/ה שמצבך חסר תקוה?　כ

23. האם את/ה חושב/ת שמצבם של אחרים טוב יותר משלך?　כ

APPENDIX 2 (continued)

‏24. האם את/ה מתרגז/ת מדברים פעוטים לעיתים תכופות? כ‏

‏25. האם מתחשק לך לבכות לעיתים תכופות? כ‏

‏26. האם יש לך קשיי ריכוז? כ‏

‏27. האם את/ה נהנה/ית לקום בבוקר? ל‏

‏28. האם את/ה מעדיף/ה להמנע ממפגשים חברתיים? כ‏

‏29. האם קל לך לקבל החלטות? ל‏

‏30. האם חשיבתך צלולה כשם שהיתה? ל‏

‏<u>הוראות העברה:</u> פורמט העברה בעל - פה עדיף עם קשישים תשושים.‏
‏על המאבחן יהיה לחזור על השאלה כדי להשיג תשובה ברורה של כן או‏
‏לא.‏
‏ה-ס.ד.ג. מאבד מתקפותו ככל שעולה שיעור הדמנטיה. ה-ס.ד.ג. עובד‏
‏היטב גם עם קבוצות גיל אחרות ועשוי להיות מתאים ביותר עם פציינטים‏
‏הסובלים מבעיות גופניות רבות.‏

‏<u>שקלול:</u> יש להעניק נקודה אחת לכל תשובה דכאונית.‏
‏10 - 0   נורמאלי‏
‏20 - 11   דכאון קל‏
‏30 - 21   דכאון בינוני עד חמור‏

APPENDIX 2 (Yiddish Version)

GERIATRIC DEPRESSION SCALE

‎.1 זענט איר אין אלגמיין צופרידן פון לעבן ?   ניין

‎.2 האט איר אויפגעגעבן אסך פון אייערער טעטיקייט און אינטערעסן ?
‎   יא

‎.3 צו פילט איר אַז דאָס לעבן איז ליידיק ? יא

‎.4 פילט איר האָפט לאנגוויייליק ?   יא

‎.5 צו האָט איר האפענונג וועגן צוקונפט ?   ניין

‎.6 צו זענט איר צעשטעיט פון מחשבות (געדאנקן) וואָס איר קענט נישט
‎   אויפהערן טראַכטן ? יא

‎.7 צו זענט איר א מיינסט פון די צייט אין א גוטע שטימונג ? ניין

‎.8 צו זאָרגט איר זיך אז עפעס שלעכט קען אייך געשען (פאסירן) ? יא

‎.9 צו זענט איר א מיינסט פון די צייט צופרידן ? ניין

‎.10 צו פילט איר זיך אומבאַהאָלפן ? יא

‎.11 זענט איר האָפט אורוהיג ? יא

‎.12 צו ווילט איר בעסער בלייבן אין שטוב וואס ארויס פון שטוב
‎   און מאַכן נייער זאַכן ? יא

‎.13 צו זאָרגט איר האָפט וועגן צוקונפט ?   יא

‎.14 פילט איר אז איר האָט פראבלעמען מיט'ן זיכרון מער פון אנדערע
‎   מענטשן ? יא

‎.15 צו טראכט איר אז עס איז זייער גוט לעבן איצט ? ניין

‎.16 פילט איר האָפט אין א שלעכט געמוט ?   יא

‎.17 צו פילט איר אז איר זענט איצט נישט גארנישט ווערט ? יא

‎.18 צו זאָרגט איר האָפט וועגן די פאַרגאַנגענהייט ? יא

‎.19 פילט איר אז לעבן איז אנטוזייאסטיש ? (פריילעד ?) ניין

‎.20 צו איז אייך שווער אָנצוהייבן מיט נייער פרויעקטן ? יא

‎.21 האָט איר אסך ענערגיע (כח) ? ניין

‎.22 צו פילט איר אז אייער מצב איז אָן האפענונג ? יא

‎.23 צו טראכט איר אז רוב (או מיינסט) מענטשן זענען און אַ בעסערער
‎   מצב פון אייך ? יא

‎.24 ווערט איר האָפט אויפגערעגט פון קליינע זאַכן ? יא

‎.25 פילט איר האָפט אז איר ווילט וויינען ? יא

‎.26 צו איז אייך שווער קונצענטרירן ?   יא

‎.27 צו האָט איר הנאה אויפשטיין אין די פרי ? ניין

‎.28 ווילט איר בעסער נישט , אינטייל-נעמען אין געזעלשאפטלעכער
‎   טרעפונגען ? יא

‎.29 צו איז אייך לייכט באַשליסן ? ניין

‎.30 זענט איר קלאר ווי איר זענט געווען אַ- מאָל ? ניין

APPENDIX 3 (Hebrew Version)

HYPOCHONDRIASIS SCALE

סולם היפוכונדריות
עיבוד ותרגום עברי: דר' אלי זומר

1. האם את/ה מרוצה מבריאותך רוב הזמן?   ל

2. האם קורה שאת/ה מרגיש/ה לגמרי בריא/ה?   ל
("חוץ מבעיה ספציפית אחת...." = כ)

3. האם את/ה עייף/ה רוב הזמן?   כ
("אני מתעייף לעיתים תכופות" = ל)

4. האם את/ה חש/ה   במיטבך בבוקר?   ל
("תמיד אני מרגיש/ה אותו דבר" = כ)

5. האם יש לך לעיתים תכופות כאבים ומחושים משונים שאותם את/ה לא
יכול/ה להסביר?   כ
(אני יודע/ת מה הכאבים שלי" = ל)

6. האם קשה לך להאמין לרופא כשהוא אומר לך שאין לך משהו שאינו
בסדר מבחינה רפואית?   כ
(הרופא יודע מה לא בסדר אצלי" = ל)

העברה: ניתן להעביר פריטים אלה בפורמט כתוב, אך לפציינטים רפואיים
עדיפה העברה בעל - פה. אם משתמשים בפורמט כתוב, יש להדפיס בדף
התשובה כן / לא לאחר כל שאלה, והנבדק מתבקש להקיף בעיגול את
התשובה הטובה יותר. אם ההעברה היא בעל - פה, על המאבחן יהיה
לעיתים לחזור על השאלה, כדי לקבל תשובה שהיא כן או לא ברורה יותר.
תשובות לא היפוכונדריות הניתנות לעיתים תכופות הוצגו לאחר השאלות
לעיל.

ציינון: מנה/י נקודה אחת לכל תשובה היפוכונדרית. קיימת אפשרות
שהפציינט יקבל ציון גבוה (לדוגמה - 6-3) ובכל אופן לא יפגין
תלונות סומטיות. כל פציינט עם מספר תלונות סומטיות, המקבל ציון
גבוה, עלול לסבול ממחלה דלוזיונית. יחד עם זאת, במבחן זה עלולים
להתקבל גם איבחונים שגויים (FALSE POSITIVES). כל ציון מתחת ל - 3
הוא בהחלט לא ציון היפוכונדרי, ואז יש להתייחס ברצינות רפואית
לתלונות.

APPENDIX 3 (Yiddish Version)

HYPOCHONDRIASIS SCALE

1. צו זענט איר צופרידן פון אייער געזונט-צושטאַנד אלגעמיין ? ניין

2. האָט איר פריער זיך געפילט אינגאַנצן געזונט ? ניין

3. זענט איר האפט מיד ? יא

4. פילט איר זיך אמבעסטן אין די פרי ? ניין

5. האט איר פון צייט צו צייט ספעציעלע ווייטיגן וואס ס'איז אייך שווער אויפקלערן ? יא

6. איז אייך שווער צו גלייבן ווען דער דאקטער זאגט אייך אז איר האָט נישט קיין פיזישע פראבלעם ? יא

Index

ABREACTION
see catharsis
ADAPTIVE MECHANISM
see defense mechanism
AFFECTIVE DISORDER
see depression
AGITATION
77,78,92,128
AGGRESSION
48,51,87,89,90,114,122
ALZHEIMER'S DISEASE
see dementia
AMNESIA
see dissociation
ANGER, ANGRY
20,23,43,44,50,56,60,,61,
85,88,92,102,106,108,109,
122,125
see also agitation,
aggression
ANOREXIA
see food
ANXIETY
7,30,32-34,45,48-50,55,
57,59,60,68,69,70,79,
80,84,92,99,100,102,
103,113,122,125,126
APPETITE
see food
APPROACH & AVOIDANCE
18
ASSERTIVENESS
49,62
ASSESSMENT
138-142
AUSCHWITZ
21,22,57,59,60,76,83,
84,89
AUTONOMY
49,101,106,112,113,
116,124,126
AVOIDANCE
17,18,23
BATH
see showers
BELZEC
11
BEREAVEMENT
1,10,11,13,22,30,47,
49,59,68,85,86,88,89,
92,97,106,109,120,125,
128,129

BIPOLAR
see manic-depression
CARDIOVASCULAR
53
CASE STUDIES
8-15,21-24,41-46,
56-61,68-71,75-80,
85-86,88-89,91,
102-115,125-130
C.A.T. SCAN
77
CATHARSIS
20,47,48,52,54,55,
59-61,90,93,107-108
CBS
see dementia
CHRONIC BRAIN SYNDROME
see dementia
CONFUSION
see dementia
COGNITIVE BEHAVIORAL
62
COGNITIVE IMPAIRMENT
see dementia
COMBAT STRESS REACTION
see post traumatic
stress disorder
COMMUNITY TREATMENT
81,96-97
COMPULSION, COMPULSIVE
22,23
CONJOINT FAMILY THERAPY
see family
CONTROL
see autonomy
COPING
5-15
COUNSELING
see psychotherapy
COUNTERTRANSFERENCE
see transference
COUPLES
see family
DANCE, DANCING
69,70
DEATH
see bereavement
DEFENSE MECHANISMS
2,17-24,43-49,53,
55,67,70,75,79,85,
92,123,127
DEHYDRATION
106

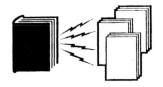

Haworth
DOCUMENT DELIVERY
SERVICE
and Local Photocopying Royalty Payment Form

This new service provides (a) a single-article order form for any article from a Haworth journal and (b) a convenient royalty payment form for local photocopying (not applicable to photocopies intended for resale).

- *Time Saving:* No running around from library to library to find a specific article.
- *Cost Effective:* All costs are kept down to a minimum.
- *Fast Delivery:* Choose from several options, including same-day FAX.
- *No Copyright Hassles:* You will be supplied by the original publisher.
- *Easy Payment:* Choose from several easy payment methods.

Open Accounts Welcome for . . .
- Library Interlibrary Loan Departments
- Library Network/Consortia Wishing to Provide Single-Article Services
- Indexing/Abstracting Services with Single Article Provision Services
- Document Provision Brokers and Freelance Information Service Providers

MAIL or *FAX* THIS ENTIRE ORDER FORM TO:

Attn: **Marianne Arnold**
Haworth Document Delivery Service
The Haworth Press, Inc.
10 Alice Street
Binghamton, NY 13904-1580

or FAX: (607) 722-1424
or CALL: 1-800-3-HAWORTH
(1-800-342-9678; 9am-5pm EST)

PLEASE SEND ME PHOTOCOPIES OF THE FOLLOWING SINGLE ARTICLES:

1) Journal Title: _____
   Vol/Issue/Year:_____Starting & Ending Pages:_____
   Article Title:_____
   _____

2) Journal Title: _____
   Vol/Issue/Year:_____Starting & Ending Pages:_____
   Article Title:_____
   _____

3) Journal Title: _____
   Vol/Issue/Year:_____Starting & Ending Pages:_____
   Article Title:_____
   _____

4) Journal Title: _____
   Vol/Issue/Year:_____Starting & Ending Pages:_____
   Article Title:_____

(See other side for Costs and Payment Information)

COSTS: Please figure your cost to order quality copies of an article.

1. Set-up charge per article: $8.00
   ($8.00 × number of separate articles)   _____

2. Photocopying charge for each article:

           1-10 pages: $1.00   _____

           11-19 pages: $3.00   _____

           20-29 pages: $5.00   _____

           30+ pages: $2.00/10 pages   _____

3. Flexicover (optional): $2.00/article   _____

4. Postage & Handling: US: $1.00 for the first article/

           $.50 each additional article   _____

         Federal Express: $25.00   _____

         Outside US: $2.00 for first article/

           $.50 each additional article _____

5. Same-day FAX service: $.35 per page   _____

6. Local Photocopying Royalty Payment: should you wish to copy the article yourself. Not intended for photocopies made for resale. $1.50 per article per copy (i.e. 10 articles x $1.50 each = $15.00)   _____

                                    GRAND TOTAL: _____

METHOD OF PAYMENT: (please check one)

❑ Check enclosed   ❑ Please ship and bill. PO # _____

                  (sorry we can ship and bill to bookstores only! All others must pre-pay)

❑ Charge to my credit card: ❑ Visa; ❑ MasterCard; ❑ American Express;

Account Number:_____ Expiration date:_____

Signature: X_____ Name: _____

Institution: _____ Address: _____

City: _____ State:_____ Zip:_____

Phone Number: _____ FAX Number: _____

MAIL or *FAX* THIS ENTIRE ORDER FORM TO:

Attn: **Marianne Arnold**
Haworth Document Delivery Service
The Haworth Press, Inc.
10 Alice Street
Binghamton, NY 13904-1580

or FAX: (607) 722-1424
or CALL: 1-800-3-HAWORTH
(1-800-342-9678; 9am-5pm EST)